Bill Tipper

FACTS ABOUT MAUI

Square Miles: 729
Acres: 466,304
Length: 48 miles
Width: 26 miles
Population: 86,900 (1985)
Distance from Honolulu: 70 miles
Distance from San Francisco: 2390 miles
Highest point: Haleakala Summit 10,023 feet

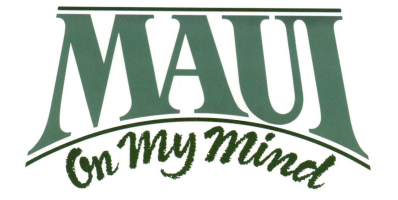

MAUI
On My Mind

Featuring the Images of
Hawaii's Finest Photographers

MAUI
On My Mind

Featuring the Images of
Hawaii's Finest Photographers

Written by Rita Ariyoshi
Designed by Bill Fong & Leo Gonzalez

Signature Publishing

Mutual Publishing of Honolulu

*Left: Brightly colored heliconia thrive in Maui's tropical
environment. —Jacob Mau/Alii Gardens.*

Special thanks and song acknowledgement
to Ken Makuakane: *Maui on My Mind*
by Kenneth Makuakane © 1982

Library of Congress catalogue card number 85-062692
ISBN: 0-935180-16-8

Produced by Bennett Hymer and David Rick

Mutual Publishing of Honolulu   Signature Publishing
2055 North King Street   1123 Kapahulu Avenue
Honolulu, Hawaii 96819   Honolulu, Hawaii 96816

Printed in Japan by Toppan Printing Company

First Edition, November 1985
Second Edition, June 1986
Third Edition, December 1986
Fourth Edition, December 1987
Fifth Edition, December 1988

Text by: Rita Ariyoshi
Art Direction and Design:
   Bill Fong and Leo Gonzalez
Design Assistants: Peter
   Matsukawa, Debra Michimoto,
   Lisa Linbo and Grover Ishii
TYPOGRAPHY
Chapter headings: Calligraphy by
   Leo Gonzalez
Text type: Garamond (ITC) Light
Text captions: Garamond (ITC)
   Light Italic
Vignette headings: Garamond
   (ITC) Condensed Book
Vignette text: Garamond (ITC)
   Condensed Light

Vignette captions: Garamond
   (ITC) Light Italic
Typesetting by: Innovative Media
   and Ad Type, Inc.
PRINTING
Cover: T-Saifu over 2000
   GSM board
Text: 4 colors on 157 GSM gloss
Endsheets: 4 colors on 157
   GSM/woodfree
Jacket: 4 colors plus film
   lamination on 128 GSM
Printed and bound in Tokyo,
   Japan, by Toppan Printing
   Co., Ltd.

Signature Publishing

Mutual Publishing

Contents

Contributing Photographers and Artists

The photographs chosen for this book were painstakingly assembled over a twelve-month period beginning with an initial selection made from the stock of photographers currently living on Maui. Additions to this first selection were then made by a review of the files of other photographers who had a special appreciation for the island. The next step was to assign photographers to shoot areas that were not yet adequately covered.

In all, over twenty thousand slides were examined, including some black and white portraits, and vintage photographs from museums and private collections. A preliminary selection of one thousand images was assembled, based on the criteria of sharpness, brightness, color density, design, and, of course, subject matter.

Making the final choice from among these excellent photographs was the most difficult step. Here, the critical eye of the designer took over. The images had to complement each other as well as fit the chapter themes. Many excellent photographs were omitted in the process.

The sizing of the images was based on the same criteria. When the design was completed, the following men and women became contributing photographers.

Erik Aeder
Rita Ariyoshi
Ray Jerome Baker (1880–1972)
Deanna Benatovich
Dennis Callan
Peter Cannon
Sylvain Cazenave
Carol Clarke
Hunton Conrad
David Cornwell
David Davis

Tami Dawson
Hugo deVries
Bill F. Eger
David Franzen
Peter French
Robert Gilman
Bill Gleasner
Warren Gouveia
Sanford Hill
Cliff Hollenbeck
Randy Hufford
Larry Ikeda
Wayne Istre
Ralph Kagehiro

Greg Kaufman (Pacific Whale Foundation)
Gaylord Kubota
Ronald Lester
Ray Mains
Craig Matsueda
Jacob Mau
Stephanie Maze
Tom Mitchell
Linny Morris
John Motelewski
Loli Nakamoto
L. Clifford Norager

Douglas Peebles
Ed Robinson
Richard Roshon
Marc Schechter
John Severson
Gary Sohler
Sherry Lee Thompson
Bill Tipper
Cindy Turner
Greg Vaughn
William Waterfall
Jon Woodhouse

Left: Acres of pineapple fields flourish on the northwest coast of Maui in the fields of the Maui Land & Pineapple Company. —Ray Mains.

Maui on My Mind is indeed a magnificent tribute to this glorious, God-blessed collection of islands that we, its residents, so proudly and gratefully acknowledge as Home.

Maui on My Mind has succeeded in depicting the beauty of our natural endowments while illustrating the life and activities of our residents and visitors.

Besides its excellent use of graphics and text, this special publication represents Maui at its best.

Maui on My Mind is special because it has been produced not only as a pictorial record of the County's attributes and charming qualities, but also to support and benefit Ka Lima O Maui, one of our important non-profit service organizations which has long provided employment and training opportunities to Maui citizens with disabilities.

As Mayor of the County of Maui, I commend the producers of this fine product since I am confident it will be enjoyed by all who obtain it, thereby providing much needed assistance to Ka Lima O Maui, the Maui Rehabilitation Center.

Aloha,

Hannibal Tavares

HANNIBAL TAVARES
Mayor, County of Maui

Left: Deserted beaches and year-round ideal weather: A Maui trademark that attracts visitors from around the world.
—John Severson.

Acknowledgements

MAUI ON MY MIND is not only the title of this book, it is a factual statement. Maui has been front and center in the minds of the many people who have participated in the book's creation. For some, the commitment stretches back several years.

The photographs in the book represent the best efforts of the best photographers in Hawaii. In search of the perfect picture, these men and women have traveled miles of Maui roads, hiked into impossible places, and leaned from precarious perches. They have been up before the dawn and were still framing images when the Maui moon sailed across the starry sky.

Choosing the photographs for the book from among the thousands of elegant and artistic images submitted was not easy. Arranging the collection in a harmonious whole with drama, simplicity, and impeccable style took countless hours of designing, redesigning, and fine tuning the graphics. Bill Fong and Leo Gonzalez of The Art Directors accomplished this with flair, grace, brilliance, and no small amount of diplomacy and patience.

Galyn Wong acted as production coordinator. Her task was to keep all the material organized and completed on schedule.

The table of contents was the suggestion of the Honorable Mayor Hannibal Tavares of Maui County. Mary C. Sanford, Nora Cooper, Bob Jones, Mae McCarter, and the staff of the *Maui News* provided invaluable assistance. Robert Gilman acted as an initial photography source and contact, introducing the work of many Maui photographers.

Will Kyselka, Lori Ackerman, and Tom Nickerson reviewed the manuscript for accuracy.

Pundy Yokouchi and Thomas S. Yagi provided valuable assistance in introducing us to the Maui community.

Special thanks are also extended to Gini Baldwin, Jacob Mau, Tau and Kerrylee Over, Peter and Claudia Cannon, Barbara Cannon, the von Tempsky family, Fred Romanchek, Merie-Ellen Mitchell, Katsugo Miho, Gaylord Kubota, The Maui Cooks, and Gaylord Wilcox.

The chapters and subject groupings were organized in a manner we hope will make it easy for readers to become acquainted with this rich and diverse island. In some cases the rules were stretched. The Road to Haleakala, The House of the Sun, Upcountry, and Mountain Ranching chapters could probably have been grouped together since they are one area, but it was felt that there was too much beautiful photography to compress into one chapter. The Middle of Maui was defined so that it went beyond the bounds of the isthmus separating East Maui from West Maui.

This book is dedicated to all who live on Maui, to those who have gone before them, to those who love the island, and those who will come to love it through the pages of MAUI ON MY MIND.

A me ke aloha pumehana,
Rita Ariyoshi

Left: Pineapple—"The King of Fruits"—is Maui's second largest agricultural crop. —David Davis.

Introduction

"When all is calm and nothing moves
When things go wrong
and nothing soothes
I feel so lonely deep inside
'Cause I've got Maui on my mind . . ."

from the song "Maui on My Mind"
written by Kenneth Makuakane and Mango

Maui, magnificent and mystical, is a visit to our planet in its youth. Haleakala, the volcano that formed the eastern end of the island, rose virginal and pristine from the ocean only a million years ago. Man was already leaving his footprints on the rest of the world. Great beasts had come and gone. In the far reaches of the Pacific Ocean, a new land was waiting.

Maui still waits. It shimmers almost like a mirage on the line of blue where sea and sky meet. From urban Oahu it beckons with a promise of serenity, adventure, and escape. People thousands of miles away hear its call and more than two million answer each year.

Maui, with its glistening beaches, forested valleys, and spectacular mountains tumbling with waterfalls, is more than a place. It is a state of mind. It is a way of living in harmony with nature and other people. Maui is a cherished heritage bequeathed by ancient kings and queens who forged a philosophy of aloha, which recognizes the holiness of all creation. Indeed, the word aloha, when taken to its roots, translates as alo, in the presence of, and ha as the breath of life, the essence, God.

People come to Maui from many backgrounds. The first Polynesian settlers braved uncharted seas seeking new land. The early European and American arrivals were primarily in pursuit of commerce. The New England missionaries came to save them all. The great immigration waves from Asia, and to a lesser extent, Europe and Puerto Rico, wanted only a chance to work and opportunity for their children.

Today's arrivals seek fun and pleasure, or peace in a quickly spinning world. They may be young lovers, or people giving themselves a mid-life reward. Some just want to be sure that earthly paradise does exist. For all of them, as it has for those who came before them, Maui works its particular magic.

This book is an invitation to share the magic, to enjoy MAUI ON MY MIND.

Left: Sunset at Olowalu through the branches of a Monkeypod tree. —John Severson.

The Road to Haleakala

CHAPTER ONE

The ancient Hawaiians named the volcanic mountain that dominates the island of Maui, Haleakala, "The House of the Sun," for in the mist of early morning it appears that the sun rises from the very depths of the crater. At day's end, the veils of wafting clouds again create illusion and the sun seems to return to sleep in the arms of the mountain.

At a height of 10,023 feet, this massive dormant volcano towers nearly a mile higher than the neighboring peaks of the West Maui Mountains. Haleakala's vast wind-sculpted summit caldera measures twenty-one miles in circumference and three thousand feet in depth. Its nineteen square miles could enclose the entire island of Manhattan and its millions of people.

No one has ever lived amidst the mysterious lunar beauty of the crater. Its awesome landscape resembles images of dead stars and volcano-pocked planets lost in the loneliness of space. Mark Twain, standing on the edge and gazing into the vast desolation of the crater, wrote, "I felt like the last Man, neglected of the judgement, and left pinnacled in mid-heaven, a forgotten relic of a vanished world."

Early Hawaiians made the arduous climb to the land above the clouds to worship their gods, quarry for stone adze heads, and hunt for birds. Today, more than 500,000 people a year drive the paved and twisted route to experience the spectacular sunrises and sunsets at the summit.

The path they travel is unlike any other highway on Earth, spiraling upward from sea level to more than ten thousand feet in forty miles. So dramatic is the climb, both in terms of life zones, and in what is seen and experienced, that the journey can be compared to driving from the subtropical latitudes of central Mexico to the frosty reaches of Alaska in two hours.

The temperature drops by three degrees Fahrenheit with every thousand feet of altitude until the five- to seven-thousand-foot level where a temperature inversion layer causes a more dramatic drop. Here, a blanket of clouds embraces the mountain although the sun may be shining both above and below the cloud layer. Once beyond this zone, the decline in temperature again becomes more gradual. Summit temperatures average from thirty-five to seventy-seven degrees Fahrenheit in summer months and twenty-six to seventy-five degrees in winter months.

The road to the top of Haleakala begins in the fields of sugarcane and pineapple that skirt the base of the mountain and stretch into the rolling foothills. The scenery changes in terrain and color at almost every bend in the road as the rolling acres of sugar and pineapple gradually surrender to the grazing lands of Maui's ranches.

Pukalani, one of the small towns dotting the slopes, is considered to be the gateway to both Haleakala and Upcountry Maui, the name given to the upper flanks of the mountain. Beyond Pukalani, acres of vegetable farms and flower nurseries adorn the hillsides. The familiar hibiscus and palms of lower elevations are replaced by hollyhocks and pines. Fragrant eucalyptus, young eighty-foot redwoods, and, surprisingly, cactus line the road.

As higher elevations are reached, clouds begin to roll over the meadows like celestial magicians, revealing only what they choose. Fences seem to be lost in infinity; horses appear like mythical creatures in the clearings, and the sun, in sudden bursts, lights the forest.

Gazing down the sides of the mountain, the plains and the silhouettes of the West Maui Mountains loom as lovely reminders of the world left behind.

Beyond the tree line, the mountain assumes a craggy solitude as the road seems to wind into a bleak eternity.

Those who know Haleakala best claim that the ideal time to visit is at dawn. Then, the first heralds of morning color roll upward, hesitantly at first, then with authority, until suddenly the eastern rim is ablaze with an intense light, ignited by La, the sun, who rises from his volcanic chamber. Only the top of the brilliant orb is visible — and then more — until finally the sun has cleared the horizon and everything comes to life. The moonscape of the crater burns in tones of rose and amber. The swirling shapes of the sand, the massive cinder cones, and the hills and crevices are alive with colors running from russet to ochre.

This magnificent spectacle is staged every day while most of the world slumbers. Joy rises like the sun itself. Night is vanquished. There is another day of life. The island, spread out below, is bathed in morning gold. Awake, Maui. ∎

Opposite: Beautiful scenery is everywhere. —David Davis.
Previous page: A drive up the road to ten thousand twenty-three foot high Haleakala is unlike any other in the world. —Ray Mains.

Above left: Ideally suited to the weather and soil conditions, huge trees line the road at the middle elevations. —David Davis. Above right: Cactus is one of the many surprises encountered along the way. —David Davis. Top: About mid-morning, clouds borne on the trade winds roll across the mountainside like clock work. —David Davis.

Above: Working in harmony, the sun and the clouds offer beautifully lit meadows. —David Davis. Top: Beef herds roaming the hills and ravines supply Maui with much of its fresh meat. —David Davis.

24

Previous page: Within one thousand feet of the summit, around the entire crater rim, herds of wild goats roam and cause great damage to the natural flora and fauna. The National Park service maintains an on-going eradication program with the help of local hunters. —Bill Tipper.

Left: Having risen before dawn to drive in the dark, a couple, wrapped in blankets against the chill, stands at the summit of the volcano awaiting the spectacular sunrise. —David Franzen. Above: After the lush lower slopes, the terrain flanking the road becomes stark above the tree line at the eight thousand five hundred foot level. —Hugo deVries. Top: The ultimate bike ride: from the ten thousand foot Haleakala summit to sea level without pedaling. This new activity attracts people of all ages. —Doug Peebles.

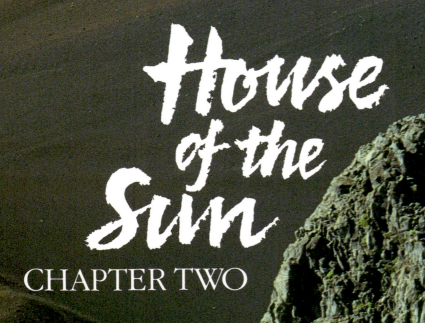

House of the Sun

CHAPTER TWO

A new chapter in the book of creation was written twenty-five million years ago. In the darkest depths of the ocean, molten lava spewed forth forming stone pillows, one mounded upon the other, building first one island of Hawaii and then another as the tectonic land plate inched northwestward over the hot spot in the Pacific Ring of Fire.

Haleakala is less than one million years old. Lava from the volcano's initial stage, the Honomanu time, can be seen along the northern coast of the island, particularly in the sea cliffs of Keanae.

During the second stage, called Kula, volcanic fires raged in spectacular outbursts. The caldera was formed, three thousand feet deep and twenty-one miles in circumference. Eruptions piled up the Kula cinder cones along the Halemauu Trail of the crater floor.

The third stage, the Hana period, formed the crater's three largest cinder cones, the highest of which, Puu o Maui, reaches nearly one thousand feet. Erosion sculpted Haleakala and defined its present height of ten thousand, twenty-three feet above sea level, with another nineteen thousand feet descending to the floor of the ocean. The Hana phase ended only eight hundred to one thousand years ago. Haleakala, the sleeping giant, last erupted in 1790.

Prehistoric Maui, which geologists refer to as Maui Nui, or Big Maui, was much larger than the Maui of today, and encompassed six major volcanic peaks that now comprise the separate islands of Molokai, Lanai, and Kahoolawe.

The Hawaiian islands are more than two thousand miles from any land mass and emerged from the ocean sterile and lifeless. Seeds and spores of plants arrived in the wind, the ocean currents, and as the gifts of migratory birds at the rate of one new species every forty thousand years. In isolation and without competition, the colonizing species evolved into a unique biota.

The first Polynesians, in their legendary voyaging canoes, carried with them new plants and animals. The impact of their arrival brought an end to much of the endemic life, which had existed nowhere else on the planet. The native forest retreated until today the mountains of the Islands, especially Haleakala, offer some of the most striking examples of the surviving plant life. One of the most spectacular is the beautiful ahinahina or silversword which

blooms once and dies. At one time, plundered and harvested with abandon, they numbered less than one hundred plants. Now under legal protection, they again cheer the desolate landscape.

The early birds that arrived on Hawaiian shores followed the same evolutionary pattern. The nene, which inhabits the crater of Haleakala, is believed to be descended from the Canadian goose. Forty years ago, the nene numbered less than fifty in the wild, and was on the brink of extinction. Under protection, it was reestablished in the crater in the 1960s. The nene fared better than the Hawaiian ibis, a large flightless bird whose skeletal remains, found near the crater, are all that is left of this species.

The impact of environmental change is obvious at Hosmer Grove, an area of introduced plant life from as far away as the Himalayas of Nepal. Native Hawaiian birds — the apapane, iiwi, and amakihi — no longer at home in the lowlands, have found a sanctuary among the foreign verdure.

The ancient Hawaiians regarded Haleakala as a sacred place. The Spectre of the Brôcken, a natural phenomenon allowing a person to see his own shadow in a halo of rainbow-hued mist, was called Aka-ku-anue-nue, "the seeing of one's own soul."

This crucible of legend is a vast silence, with only the wind and the clouds for companions. Sand and cinder cones are everywhere. Green olivine and black augite glisten like unearthly jewels from these "mountains of the moon."

The summit of Haleakala was declared a part of Hawaii Volcanoes National Park in 1916, and acquired full status of its own as a national park in 1961.

Just outside the park boundary huddles a cluster of low buildings called Science City, constructed in 1960 not only to observe the sun, but to watch the night skies for a different "angel of light" — the hydrogen bomb exploded by the United States over Johnston Island, eight hundred miles away. Off limits to visitors, it is operated jointly by several independent institutions pursuing scientific goals, including bouncing laser light beams off prisms placed on the moon by the Apollo astronauts. The round trip takes two seconds.

Haleakala can be appreciated on many levels, from the wonder of its lunarscape to its unique flora and fauna, to its spiritual dimensions. It can be touched lightly, from the rim, or it can be explored in its infinite moods and kaleidoscopic displays of temperament. ■

Opposite: The beautiful sunrises reward those who brave the early morning chill. —Rita Ariyoshi. Previous Page: Looking into Haleakala crater from the summit, the vistas have an eerie, lunaresque beauty. The usually red and ochre cinder cones have been turned green by heavy winter rains. —Hugo deVries.

Left: An early morning aerial view reveals the enormous nineteen square mile crater and the end of the road that winds up to the two observatories. —Ray Mains. Above: In dead silence hikers trek patiently across the crater floor. —Bill Tipper. Top: The Hawaiian nene goose, once an endangered species, is now protected by law and is again thriving at Haleakala. —Sanford Hill.

Declared a part of the Hawaii Volcanoes National Park in 1916 and officially designated a national park in 1961, Haleakala inspires thoughts of infinity and desolation. It yields itself to hikers, riders and helicopters. Left: Ray Mains. Above: David Franzen. Top: Peter French.

Left: A rare silversword bursts into bloom high on the summit rim with the smaller island of Lanai lying offshore in the distance. —Randy Hufford. Above: Perched on the crater rim and blessed with clear air, "Science City" facilities survey the heavens and conduct laser experiments between the earth and moon. —David Davis. Previous page: Horseback riders pause in the lush portion of the crater's interior at Paliku where overnight cabins are available by reservation with the park service. —Ray Mains.

Maui: Superman of Hawaiian Myth

In some distant dawn of enlightenment, Maui the Great One probably existed. He was, no doubt, a mortal whose heroic feats were used to inspire future generations. His deeds evolved into epic legends and both he and the stories grew in stature with each retelling.

Maui appears throughout the mythology of Polynesia as an oceanic Hercules. He is Maui the Wonder Worker who snares the sun, brings fire to man, raises islands from the ocean floor.

The details of his birth vary. All versions, however, agree that his mother was Hina, and that he was a direct descendant of Wakea, the father of all living creatures. Some say his mother set him adrift in a seaweed boat because he was born weak during a time of famine. He was taken beneath the waves and raised in the dark realm of the oceanic gods. He was given wisdom and many divine powers. The child, though, was full of mischief and used his magic for pranks and riddles. In despair, his mentors finally returned him to his mother when he was eight years old.

One story credits Maui with fishing up land from the ocean floor with a magic hook formed of an ancestral jawbone. It is said that he, or one of his brothers, looked back as the land emerged from the sea and the magic was broken. The land mass shattered into the small islands of Hawaii.

A favorite Maui story pits man against the gods in a seemingly impossible situation. While Maui is not completely victorious, he does manage to exact a compromise from the gods, which is the best to which any man can aspire.

In the early times, the days were very short and the people never had enough light to complete their tasks. Hina, who took great pride in her fine tapa work, was unable to dry her bark cloth designs in one day. Maui took it upon himself to fix things for his mother. He learned that a blind grandmother of his lived in the crater of Haleakala, in bondage to the sun god La. Victim of a love-hate fantasy, she had been blinded by the light of La. Still enthralled, she cultivated bananas and fed him the ripe fruit each morning as he rose from the night and flared over the lip of the crater.

Maui climbed to the House of the Sun. He prepared a net to snare La the very next morning. Some say the strong net was woven of ieie vine, others say olona, and some say the hair of his grandmother.

The bananas were set out as usual, and Maui began his dark vigil. He prayed to the god of the ocean to cool him, to keep cold water flowing in his veins as he fought the very source of heat. He was a solitary man standing in the night awaiting the coming of day, knowing it would be a day of battle, of testing, and in the end he would win — or die. As the sky lightened he became more alert. His muscles tightened as he gripped the net. Rays of the sun stretched out to pierce the darkness, and then, in full glory, La blazed across the sky. He paused for the offering of bananas, as was his custom. In that moment, Maui's net whistled like the wind and surrounded the sun with a snap, like a whip. The sun struggled to be free. He singed the net and little sparks raced along the fiber, but the net held. Every muscle taut, Maui prepared to cripple the sun, so La would be forced to crawl across the sky and the days would be longer for men. Desperately, the captive sun reminded Maui that the wrong blow might kill him, extinguishing all light and warmth from the world forever. "In winning," he taunted, "you will lose." Unshaken, Maui raised his ax for the maiming blow. From behind, the voice of his grandmother pleaded for mercy. He wavered. Where the sun's logic fell on deaf ears, he listened to the entreaties of the old woman, still blinded by love.

In the end, a compromise was reached between the man and the mighty sun god. La agreed to move more slowly across the sky for half the year and resume a more brisk pace for the other half. Maui released him to rise to his rightful place in the heavens. From that day forward, men had more daylight to accomplish their tasks and enjoy the earth, and Hina's tapa could dry before evening.

The night sky, too, bears the mark of Maui, for the constellation that some men call Scorpius is in actuality the magical jawbone hook that Maui used to bring up land from the ocean. It is now among the stars and is called Manaiikalani, "made fast to the heavens."

There are probably as many Maui stories as there are islands in the ocean, but there is only one island named for him, Hawaii's Maui. ■

Upcountry Maui

CHAPTER THREE

"Everything is cooler in Kula" is a local expression applied to "Upcountry" Maui, and it has as much to do with Kamakani Hau, the cold wind that blows across the higher slopes of Haleakala, as it does with the ambience of the mountainside district. This rustic enclave, once the exclusive domain of cowboys and farmers, has lately acquired an air of fashionable retreat. The Kula district, which includes all the hamlets and towns on Haleakala's upper slopes, has been called the Marin County of Hawaii.

The character of Kula is reflected in the main street of its principal town, Makawao, fifteen hundred feet high on the mountain. Older shops sell saddles, leathers, and rifles for hunting pigs, side by side with the "mom and pop" bakeries and groceries. Their new neighbors are boutiques offering hand-embroidered clothing from Bali, and batiks, artwork, and treasures from local artisans and exotic ports of call. There are horses tethered behind the stores and expensive four-wheel drives parked in front.

It was the descendants of Christian missionary families from New England who first gave Kula status. They built palatial homes that today serve as schools and art centers. The real growth of Upcountry, however, can be attributed to immigration from China, Japan, and the Portuguese islands of Madeira and the Azores. These newcomers built solid homes and inspired churches, worked the farms and ranches, and raised their children with a love of the land.

They live amid a patchwork of color, with gardens abounding in flowers ranging from the sedate "English country" variety to flamboyant tropical blooms. All thrive in the volcanic soil and cooler Kula temperatures, which average in the seventies most of the year and in the sixties at the higher elevations.

The early Hawaiians recognized the farming potential of Upcountry. They cultivated taro and sweet potatoes, later switching to Irish potatoes, when the first Yankee whaling ships came calling. The whalers would anchor in Maalaea harbor and raise a white flag, which was the signal for the Hawaiian farmers to dig up their crop, barrel it, and carry it down the mountain for trade.

During the California Gold Rush, Upcountry farmers fed the forty-niners potatoes, corn, and wheat, along with apples, peaches, plums, and pears. Without gold ever having been panned, the area became so prosperous that Upcountry was called Nu Kaliponi — New California.

The Union Army in the American Civil War went to battle dressed in uniforms of Kula cotton. The crop remained an Upcountry staple for thirty years.

Taro patches were replaced by rice paddies, and they in turn were converted to sugarcane. The sugar plantations were the foundation of all the big Upcountry ranches, including the thirty-thousand-acre Ulupalakua Ranch.

Today, Kula crops include lettuce, cabbage, turnips, tomatoes, cauliflower, cucumber, carrots, peas, the famous Kula onion, and flowers.

Upcountry blossoms are the bouquets of Europe and America. Fields of carnations wave in the breeze, along with orchids by the acre and parades of the prestigious protea.

Upcountry even grows the grape. On the lands of Ulupalakua Ranch, Tedeschi Winery nurtures fifteen acres of the Carnelian variety. After five years of gathering, crushing, and waiting, the winery has produced a very fine brut champagne, Blanc de Noirs, that was poured at President Ronald Reagan's second inauguration.

Even with bubbles from fine champagne, boutiques with old lace, and a one-hundred-fifty-acre subdivision with new homes, Upcountry, from its lower boundary at Pukalani, to the redwood heights of Poli Poli, remains essentially ranch country. The biggest event of the year is still the Makawao Rodeo, a three-day affair held over the Fourth of July weekend. When horses and riders are not roping or branding, they are often right behind the rodeo arena playing chukkers at the polo field.

Older residents cling to old ways while newcomers, drawn to the rural lifestyle, want to zone, protect, and legislate it into perpetuity. With such staunch defenders, Upcountry may not change much. It may just move closer, in spirit, to its traditional namesake — Nu Kaliponi. ■

Opposite: Upcountry living is leisurely and beautiful —Doug Peebles. Previous Page: With the peaks of the West Maui mountains looming in the distance, a horse grazes in a cloud-haunted high pasture of Olinda. —John Severson.

Left: Stands of Norfolk pine parade along the ridges, companions to forests of eucalyptus. Many species of trees and grasses were introduced by early ranchers attempting to improve the land. —David Davis. Above: Where sugar was once king, the ranches of Upcountry now reign. —David Davis. Top: Horseback riders survey the beauty of the volcanic range but horse and rider must be wary of lava rock outcroppings. —Ray Mains.

45

Left: Gently rolling hills slope upward to the volcano's summit —Hugo deVries.
Above: Interrupted only by fence posts, the pasture lands of Upcountry receive the afternoon
sun. —Doug Peebles. Top: Surrounded by moisture laden air and cooler temperatures, the scattered
ranch houses are often shrouded in mist. Though less common today many of these
homes still rely on catchment water for their daily needs. —Ronald Lester.

47

Above: Saddled and ready to ride, a horse awaits its owner beside a Makawao home trimmed in pointsettia. —Dennis Callan. Top: The center of ranching and social life for Upcountry: Makawao town. —David Davis. Previous page: The view from Upcountry is nothing short of spectacular. —Bill Tipper.

Above: At the Tedeschi Vineyards near Ulupalakua Ranch, lush grapes await harvest, the result is a fine Maui wine. — Carl Shaneff. Top: Fragrant eucalyptus trees arch across an Upcountry road. — Randy Hufford.

54
*Above: Clouds and higher altitudes bring cooler temperatures to Upcountry where
daytime temperatures in the fifties are not uncommon. —David Davis. Top: Upcountry Kula
is the vegetable cornucopia for much of Hawaii. —Cindy Turner. Right: A young pueo, the Hawaiian
owl, peacefully rests in the palm of a hand. —Ronald Lester. Previous page: Soccer practice
at Keokea Park helps make Upcountry a fun place for growing up. —Bill Eger.*

*Rural in character, ranch-oriented, gently rolling and cool,
the lands of Upcountry are a surprise on a tropical island. Left:
David Davis. Above Craig Matsueda. Top: Jon Woodhouse.*

Polo: Sport of Kings and Mauians

The first polo match in Hawaii was prompted by the post-dinner lethargy of a Christmas afternoon in Hawi, on the Big Island. Out of sheer boredom, young Louis von Tempsky, patriarch of the Maui von Tempskys, said to the men gathered around the living room, "We've told all the stories we know, eaten all we can hold, drunk more than we ought to. Let's get out of doors and have some real fun."

By fun, he meant polo: that game the British play — something like croquet on horseback, he explained. Von Tempsky had a rule book left to him by an English major in the tenth Hussars, along with six mallets and a ball. Since eight mallets were needed, the men gamely whacked two more mallets out of bamboo, fitted them with crude wooden heads — and the game was on. The untrained horses and their untrained riders, heavy with Yule cheer, played with the precision of stampeding rhinos. Everyone had a wonderful time and at the end of the game, according to von Tempsky's daughter Armine, in her book *Born in Paradise,* the toll was one broken collarbone, one dislocated wrist, two bloodied heads, seven spills, and one horse with a strained hock.

Von Tempsky dusted off his Hussar mallets again when he got to Maui, and this time the game caught on. For one thing, the Baldwins got involved, meaning that in addition to

the sport, there was the social aspect of taking lemonade and sandwiches "with the right people" between chukkers. Of course, the games had to be rescheduled from Sundays to Saturdays because the Baldwins did not play on the Sabbath, and their enthusiastic young sons — Arthur, Harry, Fred, and Frank — were practically a team in themselves.

When the paniolos, with their superb riding skills and well-trained mounts, joined in the sport, word of the fun Mauians were having with their mallets, Saturday afternoon lemonade, and "sneaky tea" spread to Oahu. Walter Dillingham, a prominent businessman always alert to social trends, jumped in the saddle, and with his battalion of sons got the game organized on Oahu. They challenged the Maui players to a game at Kapiolani Park. The Maui team and their horses set sail in a kona storm across the Molokai channel and arrived half drowned, their horses salty and water-logged, and were soundly trounced. Trouncing Maui became a tradition.

In a span of three decades, spurred by the fierce interisland competition, Hawaii's players and their mounts earned an international reputation.

The most famous polo pony in the world was Doctor William D. Baldwin's Maui-bred Carry The News. Harry Payne Whitney, East Coast socialite and premier polo sponsor, sent Baldwin a blank check for the purchase of Carry The News. Baldwin declined. Dillingham, however, had good horse sense when it came to business; the Whitney string of polo ponies was soon fleshed out with Dillingham stock, and the whole lot was proudly sent off to England for the big-time polo scene.

World War II brought polo in Hawaii to a halt as the Islands buckled down for the siege.

Years later, when the dust had settled and martial law was lifted, it took a hotelman from Chicago to get things going again. Fred Dailey happened to consider polo the greatest sport in the world, and he was determined to play. The postwar real estate boom ruled out Waikiki as a site. After much scouting, Dailey leased Dillingham land at Mokuleia for Oahu's new polo field.

To make polo more accessible to more people, Dailey changed the rules a bit. For one thing, he reduced the number of chukkers in a game from six to four, enabling a man with two good horses to play. Four-chukker games are now the rule rather than the exception on the international circuit.

Under the new rules, polo is not the rich man's sport it used to be, though it still demands as much as thirty hours a week during a season to develop the split-second timing and the crucial harmony between a player and his pony.

The new polo on Maui was captained by Peter Baldwin following in his family's bootsteps. Players sharpened their skills on the traditional interisland rivalry, rebuilding their almost forgotten reputation. Hawaii's games now attract top players and teams from around the world, including royalty, with Prince Charles of England at the top of the list.

The social side of polo is still important, and the polo names read like a social register of Island bluebloods: von Tempsky, Baldwin, Brown, Dailey, Damon, Dillingham, Glover, Judd, MacGregor, Rice, Spalding, Tongg, and Waterhouse.

The Maui Polo Club is a member of the United States Polo Association and has a regular schedule of Sunday games from April through August at the Makawao polo field. It has been called one of the most beautiful polo fields on the face of the earth, with its sweeping views down the slopes of Haleakala to the ocean. ■

Mountain Ranching

CHAPTER FOUR

The first cattle to wade ashore in Hawaii were a gift from Captain George Vancouver to Kamehameha I in 1793. The king placed a ten-year kapu on the animals, which allowed them to roam freely and increase in number. In less than fifty years, the cattle had become pests, ravaging forests and destroying farmlands. Horses, which were first brought ashore at Lahaina in 1803, made themselves equally at home on the Hawaiian range, enjoying similar royal protection.

Mexican vaqueros, whom the Hawaiians called paniolos because the word español was not harmonious with their language, were brought in to tame the wild herds and teach ranching skills to the Hawaiian cowboys.

With the whaling era came a demand for quality beef. Ranchers improved their stock by investing in breeding cattle from America. When the whalers sailed away forever, they left many ranchers stranded. Some managed to survive until the sugar boom by exporting tallow and hides.

The Reciprocity Treaty of 1876 between the Hawaiian kingdom and the United States stimulated confidence in the economic future of the Islands. Immigration increased and beef was again in demand. These factors, coupled with new laws which redistributed crown lands and permitted non-Hawaiians to own real estate, gave rise to the great ranches of today.

One of the most colorful of the early ranchers was Captain James Makee, originally skipper of a whaling ship from Maine. After leaving the port of Lahaina in 1843, he was attacked while he slept by his steward, angry over a denial of a shore leave request. With several hatchet wounds in his head, Makee subdued the assailant, headed the ship back to Lahaina for medical attention, and never left. At a creditors' auction in 1856, he purchased a sugar plantation in Upcountry. The price was not publicly specified but the *Polynesian,* newspaper of the day, said it was "thought to be unprecedentedly low." Makee built a village for the plantation workers and a mansion for himself, his wife, and eleven children. His domain included a bowling alley, billiard parlor, and Hawaii's first cement swimming pool, complete with an island of palms in the middle. Makee's reputation as a host was international, and ships from around the world docked at the Makena landing to enjoy his bountiful hospitality. In 1883, Makee closed his sugar mill and released the first cattle to roam the newly converted pasturelands of his Rose Ranch.

Today, Rose Ranch is Ulupalakua, and is landlord from the sixty-five-hundred-foot elevation of Haleakala down to the coast, and all along the shore from Kihei to Makena.

Haleakala Ranch, largest on Maui, began as Piiholo Plantation in the 1870s and continues today as a dairy farm and cattle ranch.

The Hana Ranch, on the other side of Haleakala, was born in 1945, when Paul Fagan, a San Francisco investor, cut his last sugar crop and imported herds of Herefords. To provide even more employment for the people of this isolated rural community, he built the first resort outside Waikiki. Since then, tourism and ranching have been successful partners throughout the Islands.

The ranches provide the visitor with views of wide open spaces, visions of cattle grazing in flower-studded fields, and the rustic charm of another day. Rolling emerald pasturelands flow sometimes to the very edges of the turquoise ocean and are part of the verdant green mansion that is Maui. ▪

Opposite: Introduced to Hawaii by Mexican vaqueros, ranching has a long tradition on Maui. —David Davis. Previous page: Horses frolic in the Upcountry sunset. Introduced by traders seeking royal favor, the horse multiplied in the wild under protection of the Hawaiian king. The original herds have been gradually improved by championship mainland stock. —David Cornwell.

Left: Cattle branding irons glow in the fire. —Bill Tipper. Above: For sport, cowboys ride a wild steer. —David Davis. Top: Branding operations in progress at Haleakala Ranch. —Bill Tipper. Previous page: Paniolos-cowboys of the Haleakala Ranch herd cattle at the end of a long day. —Bill Tipper.

67

Relaxing between contests a cowboy "takes five" in the chutes at the Makawao Rodeo. —David Davis. Above: Marked bulls wait in the pens. —David Davis. Top left: Held every Fourth of July weekend at the Oskie Rice arena, the Makawao rodeo is the biggest in the state. —David Davis. Top right: An aspiring paniolo watches the action. —David Davis. Previous page: Picking their way carefully through the lava rock stream bed of Waiakoa Gulch, a paniolo and his mount head homeward. —Bill Tipper.

74

Above left: A clown cavorts in the rodeo arena. —David Davis.
Above right: Miss Rodeo Hawaii reigns over the festivities. —David Davis. Top: The rodeo is preceded by a parade down the main street of Makawao town. —David Davis. Previous page: The steer roping competition is the highlight of the rodeo. A tradition of excellence in this event was established in 1908 when Upcountry paniolo Ikua Purdy traveled to distant Cheyenne, Wyoming and astonished the crowd by winning this event. —David Davis.

Above left: A young cowboy sits in the saddle before he can play baseball. —David Davis.
Above right: Mauian Inez Ashdown relaxing at the rodeo. —Wayne Istre. Top: Cowboys ride the Upcountry range as they have for generations. The traditions are passed from father to son and most modern paniolos are related by blood or close family ties. —Bill Tipper.

75

Paniolos: Hawaii's Cowboys

Cheyenne, 1908. It was a typical Wyoming summer day: Big blue sky with a dust haze softening outlines and imbuing the whole of creation with the tawny tones of the West. It was a fine day for the Frontier Day world championship rodeo. The stands were packed, the crowd excited. They were going to see their favorite cowboys in their best form. The rodeo circuit was like family, and this was the biggest reunion of the year.

They noted some strange, unfamiliar names on the program: Ikua, Kaaua. The announcer said they were from Hawaii. Hawaii? Nobody even knew there were cows in the Sandwich Islands, much less ranches. The men were as curious as their names — sun-weathered, brown-skinned men whose ready smiles were hidden in the shadows of their floppy sombreros. They wore ponchos and brightly colored shirts, gaucho-style pants, big bandanas, and gay hatbands woven from fresh flowers. They were certainly deviants from the cowboy image. They also had to borrow mounts. Spectators wondered if this was a joke.

The Hawaiians looked out over the flat Wyoming terrain that was nothing like the mountainous lava-strewn high pastureland of their islands. They figured it would be a cinch. The gong sounded for the steer-roping competition. Ikua Purdy spurred his borrowed horse; his rawhide lariat whined as it cut the air. He was off his horse and had the steer bound in fifty-six seconds flat to become the new world champion steer roper. Archie Kaaua was second and Jack Low, also

*A*ngus McPhee, colorful, controversial, and a cowhand of reputation, rode the ranges of Upcountry Maui, and later ranched on the island of Kahoolawe, prior to that island's designation as a United States military target island, used for bombing and shelling practice maneuvers. This photograph of McPhee was taken at Puunene, 1910. Left, Baker Collection-Bishop Museum. / Paniolos of Ulupalakua Ranch led a hard, often lonely life, herding stock and making long cattle drives by moonlight. c. 1910. Right, Baker-Van Dyke Collection.

of Hawaii, placed sixth.

The Hawaiians have been winning regularly at the Cheyenne rodeo ever since.

They had learned their skills well from those first vaqueros. Eager pupils, they took naturally to this art of animal handling. The men developed a brotherhood that survives to this day, with the majority of modern paniolos being related to one another. The life is hard, often lonely and dangerous, but rewarding in the extreme.

The full moon, rather than the sun, governed the early cycles of ranching. The long cattle drives would be timed so the animals could be driven by the cool silver light of the moon and stars, avoiding the heat of the day when stock weight loss would be great.

To get the Maui beef to market, the cattle had to be taken aboard interisland ships bound for Honolulu. The vaqueros devised the solution to this problem. The cattle would be driven, the day before, into open pens. At midnight, they were moved to the beach so shipping operations could begin with the first light of dawn. The paniolos, mounted on

sturdy Percherons, worked in teams. Some cattle would be fighting mad at being driven into the sea; others would be in a state of total panic. Each had to be roped and individually dragged and driven into the pounding surf at Makena. Shore boats, which were former whale boats, would be waiting just beyond the breakers. When the paniolos maneuvered the animal into position, the crew would grab the steer by the horns and strap it to a railing running the length of the boat. A loop would be tossed over the animal's snout and secured in such a way as to keep its head out of the water without restricting breathing. When the boat had five or six steer lashed to each side, it would head out to the large steamer where the animals would be hauled on board, one by one, by sling belt. In addition to the usual hazards involved in such an operation, the paniolos had to be alert for marauding sharks.

Today the cattle are trucked from the Haleakala heights to a Kahului pier where they are loaded into individual stalls on interisland barges.

The work of the paniolo has

changed with the times, and many paniolos admit they miss the silvery nights with the ghostly horned cattle moving in silhouette across the volcanic slopes. It had a mysterious beauty which is robbed by the daylight.

The stock on modern ranches is much improved with the addition of champion Mainland stock to the Hawaiian pipi. Interestingly, in the Hawaiian language the cow is called pipi while the goat is called kao, because an early explorer had promised the Hawaiians cows on his next visit. His cows died on the voyage and he was left with only goats, so they were called kaos.

While a Hawaiian ranch is now run with computerized efficiency, there is still plenty of riding, herding, cutting, branding, castrating, dehorning, and innoculating to be done — work requiring hardy men.

As long as there are ranches in Hawaii, the paniolos will be around, wearing their aloha shirts and haku hat leis, and exhibiting their award-winning horsemanship and skills.

Cries of "Ha pipi, ha pipi" will echo in the highlands of Maui for a long time to come. ■

77

Louis von Tempsky

Louis von Tempsky, a native of New Zealand who made a name for himself as manager of Maui's Haleakala Ranch, relaxes with "best friends." The life and times of the von Tempsky family were chronicled by Louis' daughter Armine in her charming book Born In Paradise, which captures the flavor of a past era of Maui. Encouraged by Jack London, a visitor to the ranch, Armine pursued her literary ambitions and immortalized her father. / Baker-Van Dyke Collection.

Mention the Haleakala Ranch, and Louis von Tempsky comes to mind, even though he never owned it.

With little more than his guitar, his charm, and a lusty zest for life, he left his native New Zealand to go around the world. He got as far as Maui, fell in love with the island, and vowed to stay. He worked as a butcher, operated a dairy and a corn mill, drove an ox team — and went on to become the manager of the Haleakala Ranch. He took the reins of the vast spread, and under his management it prospered. The Hawaiian paniolos recognized in him a man who loved the land with their same passion. They awarded him their respect and unswerving loyalty.

Louis married Amy Wodehouse, the daughter of the British ambassador to the court of Hawaii. Their ranch home, famous for its hospitality, welcomed royalty, literary lions, missionaries, and cowboys.

The von Tempsky children inherited their father's love of Maui, and daughter Armine, encouraged by Jack London, a visitor to the ranch, pursued her literary ambitions and authored several books including the popular *Born in Paradise,* a chronicle of her childhood on the range of Haleakala.

Louis' colorful father, Major Gustav Ferdinand von Tempsky, had been a political exile from Poland at the age of eighteen. As a young man he logged mahogany in the jungles of Nicaragua, mined in the California and Australia gold rushes, landed in the Yucatan, and fought under the command of Maximilian. He ended his travels in New Zealand, where he earned a reputation fighting with the English in the Maori Wars. He died in action. His second son, Louis, was heir to his untamed spirit — and not much more.

Louis' mother was of Scottish blood and had once served as governess in a prominent Maui family before going to New Zealand and marrying her handsome Polish soldier. It seemed fitting to her that one of her sons should return to Maui and achieve such prominence.

Louis, in his later years, suffered severe pain from a chronic hip injury and became increasingly disabled. When he felt he could no longer either serve life or enjoy it, he shot himself. His note to his children read, in part, "I'm . . . just another old horse sent on his way before life's a curse instead of a joy. You kids understand. Dad."

The descendants of Louis von Tempsky are many and the name is a respected one in the Islands. ■

The Hana Coast
CHAPTER FIVE

Hana is separate from the rest of Maui, set apart not just by a topographical fortress, but by boundaries of the heart.

Geographically, the Hana district stretches from Keanae to Kaupo, and spiritually from the time of the ancient gods to the present. It is described in old chants as the land of mist and the low-lying sky. The rain forests, wet with dew, cascading with mountain waterfalls and bursting with audacious blooms and ripe fruit, are present witnesses to the truth of the ages.

Contemporary bards call it "Heavenly Hana." Both descriptions fit. Hana is a place where Eden persists and where the good old days have melded into the present in a Polynesian time warp that enhances both the lives of its people and those whose moments in Hana are fleeting.

Hana's history has a dark side, too, and disaster has dropped in on many occasions. Hana's love stories are tragic and her numerous heiau, including Hawaii's largest, are bleak reminders of the severity of the old religion.

According to legend, Kauiki Head, the landmark at the right end of Hana Bay, is named for an adopted son of the Menehune, the "little people" of Hawaiian lore. Kauiki had come to the Menehune on a wave, as a gift of the ocean. He grew to be a fine young man, who unfortunately fell in love with Noenoe, the daughter of the demigod Maui. Maui forbade the union, and when the lovers defied him, he turned Kauiki into the hill, and Noenoe into the mist that comes to caress the hill each day.

At Waianapanapa, near Hana, there is a pool that seasonally turns blood red. Scientists claim the phenomenon is caused by the appearance of thousands of tiny red shrimp. The Hawaiians offer as explanation another love story. Kaakea, one of Hana's many notoriously cruel chiefs, was jealous of the affection he thought existed between his wife and her brother. Afraid of her husband, the wife ran away and hid in a cave. When Kaakea found her hiding place by sighting her reflection in a pool at the cave's entrance, he brutally murdered her. The pool turned red with her blood, as it does once a year to this day.

In the beginning of the fourteenth century, a Hana romance sparked the first interisland invasion. Two sons of Maui's King Piilani both fell in love with the same chiefess, sister of a powerful chief of the island of Hawaii. After a long and bloody siege, Hana fell to Big Island rule. It remained apart until the eighteenth century, when Maui's Kahekili finally won it back.

Before all the warfare, in the twelfth century, the Hana coast had a horrible king Hua who roasted humans in his underground imu ovens.

In more modern times, Maui's lamentable "witch hunt" happened in Hana when the Protestant missionaries became nervous over the growing number of Catholic converts on the island. When the missionaries heard that some newly converted Catholic women were holding secret prayer meetings near the Kaupo Protestant church, they petitioned a Wailuku judge to arrest them. Police dragged the Catholics from their homes, tied them together with sennit, and marched them off to Wailuku. Along the way, they preached and prayed, converting hundreds more. It became a victory march. The prisoners were greeted as martyrs, draped in leis, and awarded a hero's hospitality at every step. It took them a month to travel the ninety miles to Wailuku. When they arrived, the judge, seeing the size and festive mood of the crowd, dismissed the case.

Even sweet sugar came to Hana rudely. The first plantation operator was George Wilfong, who owned sixty acres near Kauiki. He offered ten-year labor contracts, one hundred fifty dollars cash up front, and a company store to get the cash back. When the Hawaiians declined, Wilfong brought the first Chinese laborers to Hana in 1852. His mill eventually burned and arson was suspected. More plantations were founded in the rolling hills, and by 1942, sugar dominated the economic life of the Hana coast.

In 1946, Paul Fagan brought the first tourists to Hana to stay at his ranch hotel, which is now known as the Hotel Hana-Maui. The grateful community erected a memorial stone cross on Lyons Hill in back of the hotel when Fagan died.

Hana is also home to the rich and famous. Local residents take the comings and goings of the stars in stride, awarding them an anonymity unavailable to them elsewhere. The Hasegawa General Store, in the middle of town, is often a place to glimpse the resident celebrities.

Hana is also a botanist's delight. Neighboring Kipahulu Valley is a sanctuary for many species of Hawaiian flora and birds no longer found anywhere else. The valley was added to Haleakala National Park in 1969 when the famous Seven Pools of Kipahulu, romantically but inaccurately called the Seven Sacred Pools, was threatened with development.

Hana's roads are the worst in Hawaii, and residents like it that way. Poor roads keep the traffic down. The winding Hana Highway, as it is ambitiously called, with its fifty-four one-lane bridges, was finally paved in 1969. It dips precipitously into sparkling bays foaming with surf, hugs lava cliffs, and meanders through lush forests ripe with lilikoi, bananas, mountain apple, and tumbling pristine waterfalls. It demands skill and patience, takes time, and rewards the persistent magnificently. The prize is heavenly Hana. ∎

Left: A Hana waterfall fed from the upper slopes of Haleakala tumbles through the rain forest. —Ray Mains. Above: The Hana Highway with its fifty or so miles of twisting roads affords sweeping views of ocean, jungle and waterfalls. —Cindy Turner. Top: Riders pause beside a waterfall at Kipahulu. —David Franzen.

*Above left: The Hasegawa General Store is the focus of social
activity in Hana. —David Franzen. Above right: The Hana jungles are rich in
fruit to be used by these young entrepeneurs setting up their stand. —Ray Mains. Top:
Knee-deep in Hawaiian tradition and mud, farmers tend the taro patches at Keanae. —Gary Sohler.
Right: Four-acre Alau island looms quietly behind Hana girls. The pace
of life in Hana encourages quiet times of reflection. —Ray Mains. Previous
page: A clear mountain pool fed by a waterfall at Ulaino
deep within the Hana rain forest. —Craig Matsueda.*

Left: A white cross, stark against the green jungle, commemorates early Christian evangelizers of the district. —Ray Mains. Above left: The village of Wailua lies just beyond the Keanae Peninsula. —Doug Peebles. Above right: On the way to Hana cars must cross fifty-four bridges. —David Franzen. Top: Deserted coves and shorelines lie all along the Hana Coast. —William Waterfall.

91

Heliconia, ginger, calathea and other exotics —a feast to feed growing local and mainland markets hungry for tropical flowers. Thanks to the efforts of dedicated "plant people" like Alii Chang-Alii Gardens and Howard Cooper-Helani Gardens, the Hana District has become home for many varieties of these unusual, colorful and long-lasting flowers. —Jacob Mau.

92

Above: Hana pineapple is among the sweetest on the island. —Peter French. Top right: Hotel Hana-Maui's 1920s Packards-turned-jitneys have been a Hana landmark for years, taking guests between the airport and hotel. —Douglas Peebles

Charles Lindbergh

He was only passing through. Charles Lindbergh was flying home from the Philippines and stopped to visit an old friend from the Pan Am days, Sam Pryor.

The famous aviator, who had explored most of the world, fell in love with Pryor's adopted home, Hana, specifically the Kipahulu district. He was charmed by the abundance of flowers and fruit, the gentleness of the green hills, and the warmth of the people. Pryor sold him five acres of land beside the sea, and the friends became neighbors.

With his wife, author Anne Morrow Lindbergh, he enjoyed his remaining seasons in Hana, amused by the visits of grandchildren and comforted by the sound of the ocean.

His final bout with lung cancer necessitated a stay in a New York hospital, and when the doctors concluded there was nothing more to be done, Lindbergh returned quietly to Hana.

He spent his last eight days with family and close friends at his beloved seaside chalet. He planned his entire funeral, right down to the last detail. The grave was to be lined with stones, and large enough for himself and Anne. He specified rough-hewn eucalyptus for the coffin, and said he wanted to be put in it barefoot. The headstone was to be of gray Vermont granite and of a size too big to be carried off by souvenir hunters. Lastly, his friends were to attend the funeral in their work clothes — nothing fancy.

The man who had been an international hero, almost another demigod like Maui, linking continents and flying into the face of the sun, rests beside a simple country church in the Hana district. As many as four or five hundred people a day have sought him and been inspired by the words from Psalms 139 inscribed on his headstone, ". . . if I take the wings of morning and dwell in the uttermost parts of the sea . . ." ■

In the Middle of Maui

CHAPTER SIX

Like a hammock between two upright palms, the fertile plain that earns Maui its other name, the Valley Isle, stretches between the massive slopes of Haleakala and the older, magnificently eroded West Maui Mountains.

Fields of sugarcane undulate across the isthmus in emerald waves, lapping the slopes of both sides of Maui. The first sugar venture on Maui was a mill established in 1836 by two Chinese immigrants to process the wild cane that flourished on the plain. Missionary Reverend Richard Armstrong saw sugar as a means of salvation. He wrote in 1840, "By a request of the king, I have taken some part in inducing the people about me to plant sugar cane. A fine crop of sixty or seventy acres is now on the ground ripe, and a noble watermill, set up by a China-man is about going into operation to grind it. I hope some good from this quarter. I keep one plough a-going constantly with a view to the support of schools."

The first significant commercial acreage was planted in 1863. With the opening of the Wailuku Sugar Factory in the same year, Wailuku became a thriving plantation town.

Claus Spreckles, acknowledged to be the original sugar king of Maui, arrived in 1876. He immediately proceeded to accrue to himself the land and water rights of most of central Maui. He founded the Hawaiian Commercial and Sugar Company (HC&S), and he built the most modern, efficient sugarmill in the world. Royalty came to marvel. He fell from royal favor, however, upon demanding the crown of King David Kalakaua as payment of a gambling debt. When the king borrowed money and paid the debt, Spreckles found himself shorn of leverage, and left town.

The new sugar economy held great promise for Wailuku. The prosperous town was eventually designated the county seat with jurisdiction over Maui, Molokai, Lanai, and Kahoolawe.

Neighbors only in geography, the twin cities of Kahului and Wailuku bear little sibling resemblance. Standing a mere three miles apart, their links were forged with the building of Maui's first railroad, built to haul sugarcane from Wailuku's mill to Kahului's port. Since then, the fate of the sister cities has been intertwined.

Wailuku, the older, hugs the hem of the verdant West Maui Mountains. It is hilly and green, with gardens running rampant. Its main street meanders out of town and disappears into the mist-haunted reaches of Iao Valley.

Younger, brasher Kahului is a honeycomb of subdivisions, whose tidy streets fan out on the dry scrubland, making it the largest population center on Maui.

Wailuku harbors the oldest Christian church on the island, Kaahumanu Church built in 1837. The kitchen and dining hall are all that remain of the nearby Wailuku Female Seminary, established in 1838 to instruct Hawaiian women in household skills and Christian virtues. Together with the 1841 home of the seminary's first principal, Edward Bailey, they form the Hale Hoikeike museum, housing a collection of pre-Western Hawaiian artifacts and missionary memorabilia.

The area encompassing these old buildings, and including many of the town's original wooden storefronts, has been declared a historic preservation district.

Kahului's landmarks are contemporary and utilitarian. Three major shopping malls — Maui Mall, Kaahumanu Center, and Kahului Shopping Center — parade along a half-mile strip of Kaahumanu Avenue, the four-lane main street.

The University of Hawaii, centered in Honolulu, extended its system to Kahului, establishing Maui Community College. The waters of Kahului Bay, Maui's deepwater harbor, are choppy with commerce. Ships laden with the diverse crops of the island depart, to return bearing merchandise for store shelves.

The Kahului Airport, Maui's major terminal, welcomes not only interisland carriers but also jets from faraway places, dispersing the passengers, who now number more than two million annually, to the coastal resorts of East and West Maui. Most of them never take the opportunity to discover Central Maui.

While fields of sugarcane still carpet these central plains and creep up the mountainsides, farmers with an eye to the future are now planting groves of macadamia nuts.

The isthmus that is the working governmental and commercial hub of the island, as well as its geographic center, is crisscrossed with roads linking the two distinct portions of the island, one main route going toward Lahaina and beyond, the other heading for Kihei and Wailea destinations.

The ancient Hawaiians called this land between the two Mauis Kula-o-ka-mao-mao, "the land of mirages." It still shimmers in the sunshine, belonging neither to Haleakala nor the West Maui Mountains, but is the vital heart of all Maui. ∎

Opposite: Adjacent to Maui's main airport, the towns of Wailuku and Kahului sit before the entrance to Iao Valley. — David Davis. Previous page: Seemingly boundless, the rich farmlands of the central plain connecting East and West Maui yield bountiful crops of sugarcane. — John Motelewski.

Left: The porous volcanic soils provide good aeration and hold moisture well, thus promoting good root growth in sugarcane. —Randy Hufford. Above: The central plains connect East and West Maui. —David Davis. Top: A "horse gang" controls weeds in the cane fields. —Gaylord Kubota.

Left: One of Maui's sugar mills sits in the twilight ready to convert the cane into raw sugar. Though facing an uncertain future, sugar remains an essential part of the Maui economy. —David Davis. Above: As part of an agricultural diversification effort on Maui, macadamia nut trees are now being planted in the central plains. —David Davis. Top: A cane haul truck, loaded with harvested cane, churns up dust on one of the many roads that criss-cross the fields. —Ed Robinson.

103

Maui's Tropical Plantation is an agricultural tourist attraction and is the number one visitor attraction on Maui. Visitors are invited into 120 acres of lush fields to see a variety of Hawaii's famous crops, fruits, flowers and exotics up close. The site is centrally located in famous Waikapu Valley just outside of Wailuku on Highway 30 and is on the way to Kihei, Wailea, Lahaina and Kaanapali.

Above: The Hana Highway runs through the town of Paia. — David Davis.
Top: Old wooden stores line the streets of Wailuku. — David Davis.

*Above and top: Once a thriving plantation town, and now the civic
center for the islands of Maui, Molokai and Lanai, Wailuku's winding streets lead into
the verdant West Maui mountains. —David Davis.*

107

Left: Baldwin Beach Park, outside of Kahului, is a favorite with Islanders. —David Davis. Above: Fishermen enjoy a day at the waters' edge with Iao Valley in the background. —Cliff Norager. Top: Tasty Crust has for years drawn a steady crowd of diners in Wailuku. —Linny Morris.

Mauians

CHAPTER SEVEN

Everybody loves Maui. In just one decade, between 1970 and 1980, the island's population grew by almost eighty-eight percent.

Fortunately for Maui, growth has not meant conformity. In fact, it has meant a new range of ideas and notions about what constitutes "the good life." The old Hawaiian customs are still very much in evidence in the rural areas of Hana and the West Maui Mountains where the people live simply, drawing on the bounty of the land and sea.

Working in the sugar and pineapple fields, many people are still bound to the land. The state government is experimenting with many forms of diversified agriculture to perpetuate the rural lifestyle.

The big ranches are still operating and although the range is often patrolled by jeep rather than on horseback, the paniolo way of life is very much a reality, particularly in Hana and Upcountry.

Maui's middle class lives in sprawling subdivisions from Kahului to Kula with stationwagons in the carports, and picture windows in the living room.

During the socially turbulent 1960s, Maui embraced a migration of Mainland hippies. Most eventually returned home. Others were absorbed into the mainstream of Island life; some, archaic reminders of the era, continue to live communally, earning a living at odd jobs, crafts, and even owning small businesses, most noticeably in Paia and Hana.

Many of the boutiques and stores along Front Street in Lahaina are owned by "Mainland Reborns," who, somewhere in their rites of passage, examined their lives and abruptly changed them. The former lives of many hotel busboys would surprise a casual inquirer.

There are New York and Hollywood celebrities who keep one foot in each camp, living the high life and retreating periodically to Kaanapali or Hana.

Then there are the sun-bronzed youths who have come from all over the world to follow the surf. They wait on tables by night and wait for waves in the day. Ambition extends to having a good surfboard and access to a car or a pickup truck to transport them to Slaughterhouse or Maalaea or wherever the surf is up. The girls who follow the surfers are equally bronzed and lithe. In the evening, they wear tiny tapa outfits and serve cocktails in the restaurants. When daylight comes, they don mini-bikinis and sit in the sand, waiting for their surfers to ride ashore on the next wave. It is a youth cult based on the permanence of a tan. For them, there is no tomorrow conceivable that does not involve the surfer style, and some of these youths are now forty.

Regardless of lifestyle, origins, or philosophical leanings, the lives of most Mauians are centered around the outdoors, whether "the great outdoors" involves a trek into the far reaches of Iao Valley or a day at the beach.

The waters surrounding Maui, protected by the nearby islands of Lanai, Molokai, and Kahoolawe, are excellent for sailing, surfing, and windsurfing. Colorful reef fish swim among the coral canyons and larger game fish cruise the deeper ocean.

Maui's beaches are among the best in the Island chain, and they come in colors of golden sand, white, black — even red or green sand. Bikinis can almost be color coordinated with beaches.

Life on Maui offers more choices than most tropical islands. Mauians believe they are living life in the best of all places, and they proclaim, without a trace of modesty, "Maui no ka oi," Maui is the best. ■

Opposite: A smiling Kerrylee Over and child Tai typify the youth and energy of Mauians. —David Davis. Previous page: The strong beat of the ipu drum calls to dancers of the hula. —Richard Roshon.

114

Above left: Mauians love the ocean and catching fish. —John Severson. Above right: A fisherman, cloaked in his nets heads home. —Carol Clarke. Top: The waters off Maui yield a bountiful harvest supplying residents and visitors with superb seafood. —Linny Morris. Right: Armed with nautical technology, a fishing boat goes to sea searching for tuna. —Stephanie Maze.

Above left: A tired little girl gets a piggy-back ride at the Seabury Hall crafts fair. —Linny Morris. Above right: A child becomes acquainted with many things by exploring an eclectic shop. —Linny Morris. Top: Young girls gather in their Sunday-best muumuus. —Richard Roshon.

Above: Children at a West Maui beach park "talk story." —Linny Morris. Top left: Enjoying a strawberry "shave ice" is part of the fun of growing up Maui-style. —Linny Morris. Top right: Fair-haired children of Maui live a life full of sunshine. —David Davis.

120

Above left: Kupunas-elders-dance the hula —Linny Morris. Above right: Bon
dancing occurs at Buddhist temples throughout Maui during July and August. —David
Davis. Top: Draped in flowers, ferns, vines and orchids, hula dancers await their cue. —Cliff Hollenbeck.
Previous page: Resting after a swim in the Seven Pools of Kipahulu, a young
boy warms himself on a lava rock. —Hunton Conrad.

Above: Hawaiian music is a part of the Maui lifestyle. —Wayne Istre. Top left: A student of nature has fun with a gigantic ape leaf —John Severson. Top right: Upcountry polo fan Ginny Baldwin pauses between chukkers at the Makawao polo field. Located on the slopes of Haleakala it is surely one of the most picturesque polo fields in the world. —John Jenkins.

Left: Undaunted by a shower, a child waits for her ride to school. —Linny Morris. Above: Posing after the lifeguards have gone home, a young man enjoys the view of the ocean. —Linny Morris. Top: A Maui couple showing off their hats —she wears a beautiful bougainvillea lei and he wears his own hat. —Linny Morris.

123

126

Above left: A man shows off his prize pig at Huelo, along the road to Hana. —Peter Cannon. Above right: Hula, a tradition of all the islands. —David Davis. Top: A Waianapanapa couple smiles contentedly from their window. —Jacob Mau. Previous page: Fishermen untangle the nets, retrieve their catch and prepare for the party. —Wayne Istre.

*Above: A girl gazes on her garden from her plantation-style home. —
Sherry Lee Thompson. Top left: "Paia Boy" has some fun with a squid. —Carol Clarke.
Top right: Life is good on Maui and the smiles show it. —Wayne Istre.*

127

Left: Children at play near Oluwalu with the West Maui mountains in the background. —Linny Morris. Above left: Young boys "tank up" at the Suda Snack Shop, Kihei. —Linny Morris. Above right: Touring nuns stop in the pineapple fields. —Gary Sohler. Top: Men congregate outside the Maui Senior Citizen Center. —Stephanie Maze.

*Left: The lush interior of Maui's mountains are filled with stream fed
pools which make biking into the interior a rewarding experience. — Robert Gilman.
Above: Interest in eastern religions has given rise to several religious groups on Maui. They own and
operate various businesses on the island and are responsible members of the community. —
Robert Gilman. Top: A bountiful grape harvest brings smiles to field workers
at Tedeschi Vineyards. — Suzanne Murphy.*

131

The "Mountain of the Lofty View" is a man of Maui, not a mountain. Tipping the scales at three hundred sixty pounds at the peak of his career, this esteemed son of the island rose to the pinnacles of acclaim in a discipline that is the national sport of a foreign land: sumo.

Born Jesse James Walani Kuhaulua on June 16, 1944, in a place called Happy Valley, just down the road from Wailuku, the Hawaiian baby weighed in at a bouncing ten pounds, fourteen ounces. By the seventh grade at Iao School, he was six feet, one inch tall and weighed two hundred sixty pounds. While a student at Baldwin High School, he attained his full adult height of six feet, four inches. Jesse's after-school job was with an appliance repair shop, carrying washing machines to and from the truck.

He should have been an outstanding athlete; however, he had been hit by a truck when he was in the second grade. He spent six months in the hospital and another four months in a wheelchair. His legs never regained their full strength and tired quickly. When Jesse tried out for school teams, he was always turned down.

He dreamed about football. He ran the length of the field in his sleep. Finally, Baldwin coach Larry Shishido gave him a chance. He recognized potential when he saw it. An amateur sumo wrestler, Shishido urged Kuhaulua to try the sport to strengthen his legs for football.

At the time, there were many amateur sumo clubs in Hawaii sponsored by first- and second-generation Japanese-Americans. The discipline, elaborate posturing, religious ceremonial acts, and the physical and emotional stamina required in sumo are a manifestation of traditional Japanese values and the ancient cultural virtues.

During Jesse's first year in sumo, he was selected as one of seven players to be sent to the statewide team tournament on Oahu. Although the Maui team lost, Jesse won all his bouts. He also became an outstanding football tackle and an all-star co-captain.

In 1962, under the sponsorship of

132

Combining black and white photographs with color hand-tinting,
Maui photographer Deanna Benatovich creates interesting portraits of Maui
people. Above: Hawaiian girl. —Deanna Benatovich.

Enjoying a relaxing day — Deanna Benatovich.

Above: Queen Kaahumanu and her court —Deanna Benatovich.

140

*Warren Gouveia has been capturing images of Hawaiian
children for the past sixteen years. Each portrait evokes a certain mood,
expression and mana (spirit). The eyes, especially, transmit a particular essence of feeling.
Through the faces of his family and of Hawaiian children, he shares
insights and respect for the Hawaiian culture.*

141

Warren Gouveia, the photographer of these
portraits, enjoys taking pictures of Maui children. His models
include neighbors, relatives and pupils.

West Maui Mountains...

CHAPTER EIGHT

Rainbows veil the upper slopes of the West Maui Mountains, softening outlines, painting a pastel haze that erases the boundaries where the earth ends and the heavens begin.

Above the bustle of Lahaina's old streets, and beyond the man-made splendor of Kaanapali, the green carpet of the mountains refreshes the senses with visions of deep valleys and imposing mounds that reach into misted clouds.

The West Maui Mountains are actually a single volcanic shield carved by erosion to resemble a range, which the Hawaiians called Mauna Kahala-wai. Its highest peak is Puu Kukui, the "hill of light," and at its base is one of the wettest spots on Earth, receiving four hundred inches of rain annually.

Like its twin mount Haleakala which emerged from the sea at a later time, Mauna Kahala-wai was formed in three separate volcanic stages. During the Wailuku Volcanic Series, the shield was built and the summit collapsed, forming a sunken crater. A quiet time followed, during which layers of soil gathered. The second stage was Honolua, which emitted a granite-like lava outpouring. Between this period and the final one, called Lahaina, the work of erosion was done, the streams cutting the deep canyons, while the ocean, whose level rose and fell several times during the ages, carved magnificent seacliffs.

Lahaina and Kaanapali are cradled in the lap of these great hills. An apron of sugarcane with pockets of golf courses reaches up the slopes and becomes forests of mamane, kamane, hau, treasured koa, ohia lehua with its bursts of scarlet, silver-leafed kukui, and iliahi, the sandalwood.

Lying atop the peaks of Kahala-wai is a natural likeness of a chiefess of ancient times, Lihau. Her body, chiseled by wind and rain, rests between Olowalu and Ukumehame, with her trail of stone hair flowing down to Olowalu.

Another natural carving was recognized only when a new hero emerged from the pages of history. President John F. Kennedy's craggy profile presides over the entrance to Iao Valley where many of ancient Hawaii's fallen warriors rest.

Etched into the West Maui foothills, like a giant pattern of tapa, are rows of spikey pineapples. The mountain growth appears to be combed, parted, and neatly plaited. Pineapple is the last mark of man on the landscape before the breeze-scrubbed loneliness of the dry side, where all the constraints and confinements of traffic and people, and the impositions they place upon nature, are gone. The paved road ends.

Virtually unexplored are the deep valleys that radiate out like the spokes of a wheel from Iao Valley. The second highest waterfall in the United States is here. Cloaked in both mist and mystery, it is almost impossible to reach.

The beaches are among the finest any ocean ever touched, and yet they are all but deserted, except perhaps the six bays of Piilani, close to the edge of the unknown Maui: Honokowai, Honokeana, Honokahua, Honolua, Honokohau, and Hononana. It is beyond Hononana that the traveler first tastes real freedom and senses the shadow of anxiety that is the companion of utter liberty.

It translates into practical terms: In the event of a flat tire, no one will stop; a cry for help will go unheard; there will be no signs to point the way in moments of confusion; and if the miraculous should occur, no one will be there to confirm it.

Kahakuloa Head, the "tall lord," sixty stories of wind-sculpted rock and brush, appears to be a stranger to Hawaii. It would not be surprising to find on its crest a castle for the rough sea, and the everlasting wind have given it a haunted look like the coast of Ireland, grey and mauve and sparsely green. It is the refuge of great seabirds: koae, shearwater, and the ominous frigate with its huge wing-span, looking as if it has flown in from the dawn of time.

Behind the magnificent anomaly is sacred Kahakuloa Valley, the "everlasting master," akin in spirit to Halawa on Molokai. The ancients knew this land well. There is still a village here, surrounded by taro patches. The people farm, raise pigs, pound their poi daily, and wash their laundry in the stream. It is like entering a time warp.

Along the shoreline, men still come to fish in the old way, and they still leave, according to custom, the first two fish of the catch at the shrines of Koa and Koula.

The lonely road continues in a quiet ribbon until the heights of the seacliffs give way to sand dunes, and soon the circle is complete. "Civilization" is reached.

Mauna Kahala-wai is a frontier of geography and of time. ■

Opposite: Once active volcanoes, the West Maui Mountains are now covered with foliage. —Bill Eger. Previous page: Fed by rainfall deep within the valley interiors, huge rainbows are a common afternoon sight from Lahaina. —David Davis.

*Left: The morning moon still sails across the sky over the fields of sugarcane.
—Jon Woodhouse. Above: At their highest point, the West Maui Mountains reach five
thousand seven hundred and eighty-eight feet —slightly more than half that of ten
thousand and twenty-three foot Haleakala. —Randy Hufford.*

147

Left: Waterfalls drench the verdant valleys with rainfall exceeding four hundred inches per year in some areas. —Tami Dawson. Above: Rainbows seem to be everywhere. — Tom Mitchell. Top: Clouds hug the mountains. —John Severson.

Left: Just outside of Lahaina, the Pioneer Sugar Mill sits between mountain and ocean. —Eric Aeder. Above: The hillsides are deeply and dramatically eroded. —Ray Mains. Top: Agriculture creates a multi-hued quilt blanketing the lower slopes of the mountains. —Hugo deVries.

Left: Farmlands skirt the sea along the West Maui coastline. —John Motelewski.
Above: Lahaina, the former capital of the Hawaiian kingdom, is nestled at the foot of the
West Maui Mountains. —Hugo deVries. Top: Mala Wharf lies between Lahaina and
Kaanapali. —Ed Robinson. Previous page: A cane burning operation sends
smoke into the air, which is carried away by the tradewinds. —Erik Aeder.

155

Iao Valley

Into the dark folds of Iao Valley, where the walls are so steep that they have never seen a sunrise or a sunset, the ancient Hawaiians carried their departed alii and buried their bones in reverence and in secret. Few places in Hawaii are more sacred than this "Valley of the Kings."

It took ten thousand human lifetimes to form Iao, for the streams to cut so deeply into the heart of Mauna Kahala-wai, for the rain to so dramatically carve the walls, for the distinctive "needle" to assume its remarkable twelve-hundred-foot thrust, piercing the mist that glides in ghostly vapors between the forested walls.

There are moonstones in the stream bed and wild orchids along the banks. The damp trail leads through stands of tree fern, ti, and ohia and ends, finally, in a natural amphitheatre that marks the head of the valley. The

floor of this remarkable notch in the mountains is more than two thousand feet above sea level.

Mark Twain, in a euphoric moment, called Iao the "Yosemite of the Pacific." Robert Louis Stevenson, enchanted by the dew-touched verdure, could not think of an appropriate adjective to properly describe what he beheld, so he coined his own word, calling it "viridescent."

Satisfied with a view of the Needle, most people miss the real beauty of Iao. Easily followed trails lead to quiet places of meditation, with birdsong to accompany lofty thoughts. Two hundred years ago, the peace of the Valley of the Kings was shattered by a strange thunder, when the forces of Big Island chief Kamehameha swept across the plains, pursuing the army of Maui's chief Kalanikupule. The conqueror

Iao Valley, the site of some of Maui's most beautiful scenery attracts nature lovers, artists, and students of Hawaiian history and culture. Located above Wailuku town and easily accessible by auto it is possible to spend days exploring the natural beauty. It is the site of a famous battle in Hawaii's history where the forces of Big Island chief Kamehameha defeated the army of Maui's chief Kalanikupule.
— Photos by David Davis.

was accompanied by the dreaded feathered image of his war god Kukailimoku, and by the terrible new weapon salvaged from the ship *Eleanora* — cannon.

The Maui defenders held out for two days at Wailuku, then were forced to retreat into their sacred Iao. For the first time a Hawaiian valley reverberated with the roar of modern

destruction. The battle exacted such a terrible toll that it was called Kepaniwai, "the damming of the waters," for so many men were killed that their bodies choked the stream and the Wailuku River ran red with blood. The king and his retinue escaped over the mountains to Olowalu and fled to Oahu, leaving Maui to Kamehameha.

Years later, a sea captain, Gilbert Pendleton, Jr., visited Iao and penned in his log of June 14, 1846, "The Place is Covered with humane bones

for the Space of half an archer square . . . To judge from appearance I should think there was many thousand killed and thrown together in heaps."

Lovely Kepaniwai Heritage Gardens at the entrance to Iao Valley State Park carries the name of that significant battle. Dedicated to the various ethnic groups that today form the population of Maui, it is a site of pavilions and gardens, each of

which might have been lifted, intact, from the homelands.

Iao, Supreme Above the Clouds, Valley of the Kings, Yosemite of the Pacific — it does not matter what name is given. Embraced by the walls of Puu Kukui, the "hill of light," it is sacred ground, blessed with an abundance of beauty and baptized by the bones and deeds of Maui's greatest heroes. ∎

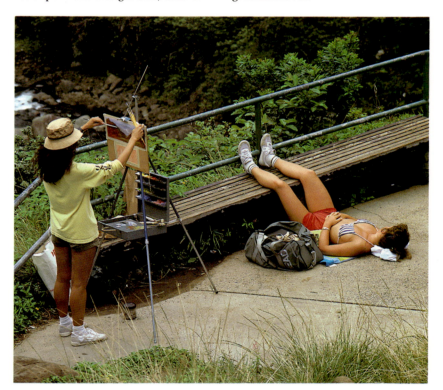

Maui Yesterdays'

CHAPTER NINE

Na keiki hanau o ka aina, "the children born of the land of Hawaii," are the sons and daughters of many races who inherit a haku lei of traditions woven into a loving embrace. The first air to enter their tiny lungs is scented with thousands of blossoms, and their life expectancy is years longer than most.

Mauians reflect the cosmopolitan characteristics of all of Hawaii. With interracial marriages exceeding fifty percent, in generations to come the children of the Islands will again be one race, a golden blend of East and West.

The Polynesians, who were the first settlers of the island of Maui, arrived in their great double-hulled voyaging canoes, sailing across thousands of miles of uncharted seas. Guided by the wind, the stars, and ocean currents, they used sophisticated navigational skills developed during centuries of exploring the vast reaches of Oceania, settling first one group of Pacific islands and then another. Hawaii was the end of a ten-thousand-year voyage. Accounts of the heroics of these epic voyages of discovery are preserved in the ancient chants and hulas. They are on a parallel with the tales of Homer's *Odyssey.*

Since there was no written language, and the tropical climate destroyed any material evidence of the ships necessary to successfully make these fantastic voyages, scholars tended to relegate the tales to the category of legend. At best, they concluded, the Hawaiians drifted on rafts in the ocean currents, landing by chance in the Islands.

In 1981, on the island of Huahine in the Tahitian Islands, a plank from an eighty-foot canoe was unearthed, along with a thirty-five-foot mast and a twelve-foot paddle. Excavations conducted by Honolulu's Bishop Museum revealed that the site had been covered by a tidal wave nine centuries before Western contact. The receding waters deposited sand and water-logged silt in just the right mixture to preserve the artifacts. Just as the legends had stated, the area, which is now being called the Polynesian Pompeii, had been the center of an ancient shipbuilding industry. Evidence now supported what the Hawaiians knew to be true all along.

The first wave of immigrants came from the Marquesas Islands in A.D. 500 to 750, and the second from the Tahitian Islands between A.D. 900 and 1300. For some reason, probably a desire on the part of the colonists for political autonomy, the voyages between Hawaii and Tahiti ceased before the arrival of the British Captain James Cook in 1778. Everything changed with Cook. New customs, new people came as inexorably as the tide.

The Americans, primarily New England sailors and missionaries, brought both sin and salvation. Their impact on the Hawaiian way of life was far greater than their numbers might indicate. From the time of Cook's arrival until 1847, fewer than two hundred Caucasians had settled in the Islands. A few Chinese had arrived on trading ships and stayed, marrying Hawaiian women, taking part in early sugar ventures, and becoming merchants. The first contract laborers from Kwangtung, China, came to work the sugar plantations in 1852.

The Japanese began immigrating in large numbers in 1885 under labor contracts negotiated by King David Kalakaua and Emperor Meiji of Japan. It is believed, that as early as the thirteenth century a crew of Japanese sailors was shipwrecked on Maui.

The Portuguese came between 1878 and 1887, the Puerto Ricans during 1900 and 1901, and the Koreans between 1903 and 1905. The immigration of Filipinos began at the turn of the century and continues until the present.

Statehood, in 1959, greatly altered the complexion of Hawaii. Between 1965 and 1970, one-quarter of the population had moved from the mainland United States.

Because Hawaii is a small island state, interracial harmony is necessary. Because the bloodlines are so mixed, it becomes natural. Because the children are so loved, it is joy. When asked about their racial extraction, most people will likely respond laughingly, "Chop suey." ■

---

*M*anager of Wailuku's Maui Hotel, W.H. Field, and his family are ready for a Sunday drive c.1911-Opening Spread, Baker Collection-Bishop Museum. / Social gathering at Spreckels Dam in Waihee Valley, c. 1890's-Opposite, Hawaii State Archives.

164

*L*ower Main Street, Wailuku, c. 1900-
Above, Maui Historical Society. / Girls from Maunaolu Seminary relaxing, c. 1912-
Below, Baker Collection-Bishop Museum. / Street scene in Wailuku early 1940s. A sharp contrast to
the 1900s.-Opposite Page Above, Hawaii State Archives. / Fish market in Lahaina, c. 1912-Opposite Page
Below, Baker Collection-Bishop Museum.

614 Wailuku, Maui

*M*aui Hotel, Wailuku, c.1915, Maui's
visitor industry has changed considerably since then.-Above, Baker Collection-Bishop
Museum. / Selling mangoes in Lahaina, 1915-Below Left, Baker Collection-Bishop Museum. /
Hawaiian canoe near Lahaina, c.1915-Bottom Right, Baker Collection-Bishop Museum.

*K*indergarten class in Lahaina. One
little girl chose not to join the group.-Above, Baker Collection-Bishop Museum. / This is
not an old photograph but still a reminder of yesterdays and todays. Hawaiian man playing music
using a washtub bass, c.1970 s-Bottom Left, Larry Ikeda. / Miss Choy, school teacher, c.1915-Bottom Right,
Baker Collection-Bishop Museum.

Plantation Days

Plantation life was hard: The hours were long, the wages low, and the work grueling. For the 184,000 immigrants who arrived between 1854 and 1905, it was opportunity. With little more than a willow basket of belongings, they came down the gangplanks of ships, hoping to make their fortunes in Hawaii's sugar fields and return home, wealthier and wiser. Some did. Most stayed, fulfilled their labor contracts, and moved on to other businesses, adding richness to the multitextured tapestry of Island life.

The plantation paid the fare to Hawaii, doled out a wage, provided the basic necessities of life, and in the end paid the fare home or provided a free coffin.

Since most workers did not plan to stay, few brought their families. Some married Hawaiian women; others, particularly the Japanese, sent for "picture brides." The prospective bride and groom, by mutual family agreement, would exchange pictures; upon family consent and registration of the brides name in the groom's family register, the young girl would depart for Hawaii. She would meet her husband for the first time at the immigration station in Honolulu, be whisked to a Buddhist or Shinto shrine for a blessing of the union, and then it was off to the plantation camp.

On Maui, as elsewhere in the Islands, the women worked in the fields beside the men, often with their babies strapped to their backs. Everyone worked. Young children baked; raised ducks, rabbits, and chickens for the table; tended the family vegetable garden; and sewed clothing from flour, sugar, and rice sacks. Often they were in the fields beside their elders by age eight or nine. Although education was encouraged, families often needed the extra wages of the children, and schooling would happen in the evening.

The plantation camp was a cohesive unit, with each nationality maintaining a separate identity within the larger unit. The people depended on one another for mutual support in times of distress, comfort in sorrow, and companionship in joy. They attended one another in birth and death and all the times in between.

In 1985, Hawaii celebrated the the one hundredth anniversary of Kanyaku Imin, the first nine hundred and forty contract laborers to arrive from Japan aboard the *City of Tokio.*

Looking back, most Islanders today are humbly grateful for the hard work, the endurance, and the spirit of their forbears, who worked in the cane fields and bought with their lives and labor golden opportunity for their children. ■

*P*uunene Mill, c.1905-Large Photo,
Alexander and Baldwin Sugar Museum. /
A plantation family, the Tobas in front of their McGerrow Camp house, Puunene, 1917-Small
Photo, Photo by Kawano, Alexander and Baldwin Sugar Museum.

*P*ayday for H.C. & S. workers, Puunene-
Large Photo, Maui Historical Society. / Camp 5 store, Puunene. The manger of this
plantation owned and operated store was Jirokichi Fujiyoshi (third from the right in the front row).-
Small Photo, Alexander and Baldwin Sugar Museum.

Cash store, Kahului, 1907-Bottom
Photo, Hawaii State Archives. / Hawaii's swim team which was the 1940 U.S. Men's
Outdoor Champions. They were coached by the legendary Soichi Sakamoto. Lacking a swimming
pool, the swimmers trained in the Camp 5 plantation ditch in Puunene.-Left, Alexander and Baldwin
Sugar Museum. / Wedding day for Mr. and Mrs. Matsui in Hospital Camp, Puunene, 1919-
Right, Photo by Kawano, Alexander and Baldwin Sugar Museum.

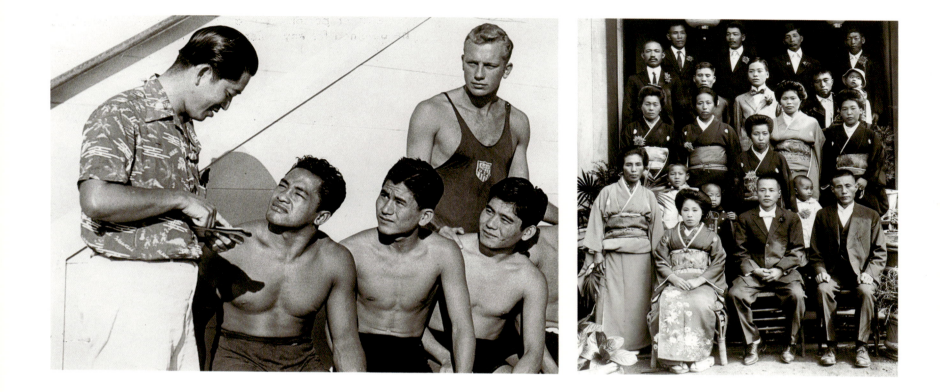

*Maui Sugar workers used to "punch-in"
on time clocks like this one.-Left, Hawaii State Archives. / Puunene School graduating
class of 1923.-Right, Alexander and Baldwin Sugar Museum.*

Flora and Fragrance

CHAPTER TEN

To remind men that life lasts but a few seasons, to disappear like the summer grass, the loveliest things in creation are the most fragile.

Flowers are like love, ultimately a gift of time and place, sometimes sprouting up in surprising settings, sometimes blooming beside the backdoor.

To the Hawaiians of old, flowers were such treasures that the word for flower, "pua," was often used to mean child. The reference is heard in the ancient chants and danced in the hula.

Flowers were woven into exquisite leis and worn as jewelry. The perishability of the lei never dictated the amount of care and artistry that was invested in it. Leis remain the most visible expression of Hawaiian culture and, indeed, are almost synonymous with the word Hawaii. They are given upon arrival and departure, for birthdays and special occasions. Leis are bestowed with love, with a kiss and the word aloha upon the lips.

Flowers had come to Hawaii long before man. Carried in the wings of birds, borne in the jetstreams, the seeds arrived, took root, and bloomed. Unseen and in utter isolation, they developed along new lines and became unlike any of their earthly cousins. These pioneering species were joined by the plants that the first Polynesians brought with them on the long ocean voyages, to plant prayerfully in the soil of the new land. Later settlers brought with them treasured flowers from gardens they would never see again. Most flourished in the rich volcanic soil, kissed by the sun and cooled by the breezes. Today the gardens and forests, roadways, and even freeways are blessed with these blossoms.

The rain forests of Maui, especially in the Hana district, are a profusion of tropical flora, the audacious heliconia and improbable torch ginger asserting themselves boldly among the ferns and trees. The slopes of Haleakala are host to flowers of the temperate zone with frontyard gardens that might have been transplanted in whole from the Mainland United States. Here, flowers are not just for fancy—they're a big, beautiful business. Orchids, anthuriums, and the strange protea, a late arrival from South Africa whose lunaresque beauty has quickly made it the prestige flower of Hawaii are exported to points around the globe.

Seven hundred species of plants grow happily together at the Kula Botanical Gardens, amid a setting of waterfalls, streams, great trees, and walking trails.

In Hana, several private gardens welcome visitors, gladly sharing the bounty that nature has so generously awarded them.

Flowers are everywhere on Maui, in bouquets and leis, even in the mai tais and beside the lettuce on luncheon salad plates. Often there will be orchids resting on the hotel pillows at night.

The Maui air is full of their fragrance, and the scent will be a haunting memory for a lifetime, even carrying far beyond Maui's shores. Traces will come back someday in the perfume of a beautiful woman as she passes quickly in a crowded room, or it will waft elusively in a summer breeze and be gone. Suddenly Maui will be on the mind again, so powerful is the fragile flower, the child of the Islands. ■

Opposite: The Upcountry climate is ideal for the protea as well as many other varieties of flowers. —Gary Sohler. Previous page: The huge protea, a native of South Africa, has become Maui's prestige bloom. —Gary Sohler.

Left: Pink hanging heliconia hides in the shade of a Hana garden. —Jacob Mau/Alii Gardens. Above left: Hanako Hashimoto harvests a gargantuan bouquet of protea from her Kula farm. —John Severson. Above right: Bromeliads, introduced to Hawaii, have found a happy home. —Jacob Mau/Alii Gardens. Top: Looking more like flowers from the moon than the earth, protea exports have become a significant part of the Maui economy. —Douglas Peebles.

181

182

Above: Dew gilds the protea in early morning. —Gary Sohler. Top left: Pincusion protea climb an Upcountry fence. —Gary Sohler. Top right; Volunteer flower vendor works at the fundraising craft fair for Seabury Hall School in Makawao. —Linny Morris.

*Above left: The brilliant lobster claw heliconia brightens the rain forest.
—Jacob Mau / Alii Gardens. Above right: Worker harvests snap dragons which thrive in Kula's
cooler temperatures. —Gary Sohler. Top: Auratiaca heliconia bursts into bloom
in Hana. —Jacob Mau / Alii Gardens.*

183

Left: Green ice plant. —Jacob Mau/Alii Gardens. Above left: Flava Christmas heliconia. —Jacob Mau/Alii Gardens. Above right: Wagneriana heliconia. —Jacob Mau/Alii Gardens. Top: Flower filled meadows dot the Maui landscape. —Cindy Turner.

185

Lahaina:
Past Meets Present
CHAPTER ELEVEN

Sailing on the wings of the wind, the Yankee whaling fleet came. The names on their transoms read *Marie Theresa, Adeline, Pantheon*. They had rounded Cape Horn in pursuit of the greatest ocean creature, the giant sperm whale, whose oil would light the lamps of the world. Long, lonely months aboard ship, punctuated by the highs of the hunt, grew into years, and when the ships dropped anchor in Hawaiian waters, the whalemen flocked ashore, the majority seeking whiskey and women, while others were content with just some steady ground beneath their feet.

Lahaina, with its clusters of fine grass houses, had, since 1802, been the capital of the newly united Hawaiian kingdom. Ruled by the Kamehamehas, its approximately twenty-four hundred residents were engaged in fishing, farming, and foresting for the China sandalwood trade. They outfitted visiting ships with a seemingly inexhaustible supply of fresh water, vegetables, fruit, beef, and hogs. Within a short time, they were tailoring their agricultural produce and other commodities to the tastes of the foreigners, abandoning yams for Irish potatoes and later even converting the royal taro patch in the center of Lahaina into the notorious Pioneer Inn.

The first American whaler, the *Balena,* out of New Bedford, sailed into Lahaina on October 1, 1819. The Hawaiians had buried Kamehameha I that year, and they had watched, first in horror and then in delighted astonishment, as his widow Kaahumanu persuaded the new King to break the ancient Kapu against men and women eating together by dining in public. The whole system of religious law came tumbling down. The stones of the heiau were pulled apart and the tikis burned while people of firmer faith wept and prayed.

On distant shores in faraway New England, a group of stalwart missionaries were "answering the call," and set sail that same year to "bring the heathens to the mansions of eternal blessedness." They would reach Maui in 1823.

During those four years the reputation of Lahaina spread rapidly and the port became the bawdy center of the Pacific whaling industry.

The harbor became a forest of masts. During 1846, the peak whaling year, four hundred and twenty nine whalers were berthed, spilling as many as fifteen hundred sailors ashore at a time. Most of them considered that there was no God west of the Horn and conducted themselves accordingly. One of those sailors, Herman Melville, immortalized the era in his classic tale, *Moby Dick.*

Concerned about the effects of the whalemen upon her people, Queen Kaahumanu invited Honolulu's missionary contingent to come to Maui. The Reverends William Richards and Charles Stewart, along with their wives, were greeted by Kaahumanu and the queen mother Keopuolani in May 1823. By October, the first Christian church on the island, a thatched building, was dedicated.

The missionaries proceeded to influence every aspect of Island life and became advisors to the royal court. In an effort to control the lusty behavior of the whalemen, they successfully lobbied for laws prohibiting everything from spitting in the streets to fornication anyplace.

The captains of the whalers divided into two camps. Those primarily of Quaker persuasion praised Hoapili, governor of Maui, "We do not any of us like to go to Oahu, because bad men sell rum to our seamen. We like your island because you have a good law preventing the sale of this poison."

Others angrily pointed out, "The life of a sailor is one of hardship and toil, and upon his arrival at your port, he needs rest and relaxation."

The first serious riot broke out in 1825 when the men of the British whaler *Daniel* learned that women could no longer visit the ships. They threatened the lives of the missionaries, whom they blamed for their deprivations. Hostilities escalated in 1827 when another English whaler fired its cannons at the Richards' home. In response, Queen Keopuolani installed cannons along the Lahaina waterfront, trained seaward.

Hoping to elevate the spirits of the sailors on something other than demon rum, the missionaries appropriated two hundred dollars and successfully solicited contributions from the ship captains to build the Masters' and Mates' Reading Room, and a seaman's chapel and reading room.

Concerned not only with present problems, but with the future of the people they had embraced, the missionaries in 1831 established Lahainaluna, the first high school west of the Rocky Mountains, to educate Hawaiian teachers. Among the first students was thirty-eight-year-old David Malo, who became one of Hawaii's noted historians. California families sent their children to Lahainaluna during the Gold Rush era.

With the decline of the whaling business, Lahaina was eclipsed by Honolulu, and in 1843, the royal capital was officially moved to Oahu. Lahaina then went into a long slumber, surviving as a neglected relic of the past, a tropical town on a sunny beach. Today it is again a port of pleasure. ∎

Opposite: Lahaina from the air. —Hugo deVries. Previous page: During the whaling days, the harbor of Lahaina was described as a forest of masts. Today it is home port to an armada of pleasure, fishing, and whale watching boats. —David Davis.

Left: The Amitabha Buddha of the Lahaina Jodo Mission is the largest Buddha outside Asia. —Greg Vaughn. Above left: A ship's figurehead brings back days of sailing brigs and lusty men. —Bill Gleasner. Above right: Lahaina is the foremost contemporary center for the traditional American art of scrimshaw. —Tom Mitchell. Top: Grinning captain of another era looks out to sea from the porch of the Pioneer Inn. —David Cornwell.

192

Above: A lei vendor sells his jewels of the fields to evening passers-by. —Linny Morris.
Top: Lahaina is a gathering place for young people from around the world. —David Davis.
Right: The old wooden waterfront stores of Front Street were declared part of a
National Historic Preservation Area in 1962. —Tami Dawson.

Left: The recently restored Wo Hing Society Building still hosts meetings and services. —Peter French. Above: The historic Pioneer Inn built in 1901 presides over the waterfront at Town Square. —David Davis. Top: Baldwin House, built in 1832, is now a museum housing missionary memorabilia. It is Maui's oldest building. —Peter French.

195

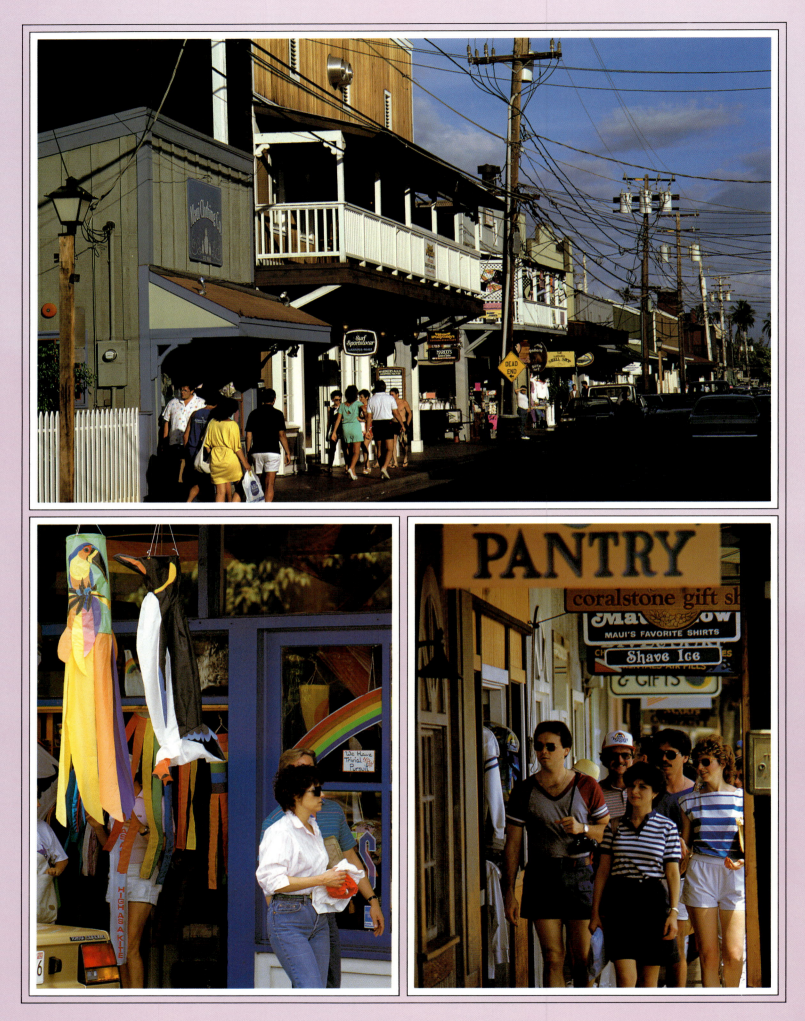

The shops and restaurants of Front Street draw shoppers, people watchers and visitors from resorts around the island. —Above left and right: David Franzen. Top: David Davis.

Above: Numbered among the pleasure boats offering tour excursions is a fifty-two-foot Chinese junk. —Cliff Norager. Top: The largest banyan tree in Hawaii was planted in 1873 in loving memory of the early New England missionaries who labored at Lahaina. —Peter French.

197

Old Lahaina

*E*arly view of Lahaina area. The
whaling boats have arrived. Artist is Nicholas Webber.-Large Photo, The Whaling
Museum, New Bedford, Massachusetts. / Waterfront, 1910.-Lower Left, Baker Collection-Bishop
Museum. / The Wo Hing Society social hall on Front Street. The seventy-two year old building dates back to
a period when the Chinese represented a major element in the community. The structure has recently
been restored by the Lahaina Restoration Foundation.-Lower Right, Hawaii State Archives.

The weathered wooden buildings that loiter along Front Street were declared a National Historic District in 1962. These gallant survivors of Lahaina's lusty whaling days, who were never beautiful even in their youth, found themselves suddenly chic. Given facelifts and new paint, their termite-eaten boards replaced and New England-style dressing introduced in keeping with their aesthetic origins, they acquired a certain patina bordering on grace.

The grog shops have long been closed and in their place are seafood restaurants where demon rum comes in mai tais with little paper parasols planted in wedges of pineapple. The ship chandlers' offices, the outfitters, the marine supply shops are gone. But boutiques offering a myriad of bikinis, batiks, and hand-painted, Maui-made clothing are prospering.

The center of modern Lahaina is the Town Square, dominated by the Pioneer Inn overlooking the harbor. Where whaling ships once laid anchor, a fleet of pleasure boats bobs — glass-bottom boats for touring the coral beds, sunset sails, dinner cruises, charter fishing boats, and diving excursion craft. The brig

199

Carthaginian II, replica of a Yankee whaler, is moored in front of the inn and serves as a whaling museum.

The cannons that once sounded curfew and marshalled the sailors back to their ships are still trained on the harbor, next to the reconstructed remnants of the old fort. The court house, whose walls have heard many a nasty tale, now dispenses parking violations and cradles an art gallery.

The largest banyan tree in Hawaii spreads its lustrous branches over two-thirds of an acre of the square. Planted in 1873 as a fifty-year memorial to the arrival of the American Protestant missionaries at Lahaina, it is home to hundreds of mynah birds whose cacophony of sermons are broadcast daily at sunrise and sunset. Oldtimers say it sounds like the same old fire and brimstone.

The Baldwin House, oldest house on Maui, built in 1832, is a classic example of how the transported New Englanders built their Hawaiian homes. With an eye for the familiar restrained lines of the Northeast, they added broad upper and lower porches, which evolved into the Hawaiian lanai.

For many a Yankee whaleman, home away from home was the Hale Paahao, the prison, with its massive coral walls standing since 1851. The name, literally translated, means "stuck-in-irons house."

Ironically, the object of the hunt, the whale, still frolics in the offshore waters, now a cetacean sanctuary, a safe spawning ground. The great humpback whale comes for the same reasons his pursuers once did — rest, play, and a measure of romance. In the winter months, the spouting and breaching of the whale is a common Lahaina sight, even from the surfside cocktail lounges.

Lahaina today might well be called Hawaii's Williamsburg except that it is a living, vital relic embracing commerce and tourism. The architecture is still predominantly New England style, much of it carefully preserved and restored, the rest meticulously copied.

People accept the landmark Pioneer Sugar Mill, and even the enormous bronze Buddha that towers over the Lahaina Jodo Mission is regarded as belonging. But to find tidy Yankee buildings with sitting porches, widow's walks, and weather vanes is a delightful incongruity. Lahaina is a surprise among the palm trees. ∎

*L*ahaina's peaceful waterfront in
the early 1900's. The Hop Wo store front still exists today and is operated by a third
generation Chinese family.-Large Photo, Maui Historical Society. / A view of the other side of
Lahaina town at the turn of the century.-Below Right, Hawaii State Archives.

202

*T*he U.S. Pacific Fleet lies anchored in
the "Lahaina Roads" during one of its frequent visits to Lahaina prior to World War II.
-Below Right. / Hula dancers entertaining the visiting sailors. Then, as now, hula was a fascinating
visitor attraction.-Large Photo and Below Middle. / A.J.A. (Americans of Japanese Ancestry) inductees from
the Lahaina area. The regiment they joined was the most decorated combat group in the
entire U.S. military during World War II. March 25, 1943.-Below Left. All photos
Nakamoto Art Studio.

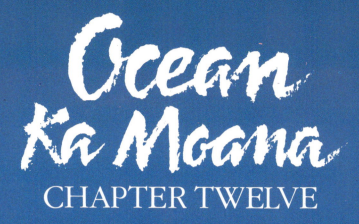

Ocean
Ka Moana

CHAPTER TWELVE

"In Hawaii, all horizons are the ocean, stretching as far as imagination will go, and all boundaries are the ocean, the end of every road."

The ocean was the crucible of Hawaiian life, bringing forth land from the depths, island by island. And the ocean is not yet finished. New volcanoes are, even now, quietly building new islands beneath the waves, islands that will one day break into daylight, support life, and be given a name that men now living will never hear.

The story of the Hawaiians and the ocean is one of the greatest stories that has never been told. Long before the fall of Troy, when European sailors were hugging the coastlines, afraid they might fall off the face of the flat earth, the Polynesians, some of whose descendants would become Hawaiians, were exploring the vast reached of the Pacific and populating new worlds. The ocean shaped these early Polynesians more than the land. Only the largest and strongest, those with fat to spare, survived the long sea voyages. Once most of the Pacific had been settled, and apparently by choice, these voyages ceased thus isolating the Hawaiians from other Polynesians and the rest of the world.

The ocean was the source of food that gave life, and it was the path of conquest plied by huge and terrible armadas of war canoes delivering death.

The Hawaiians not only met the ocean on its own terms, learning the subtle secrets of winds and currents, but they also respected it, placing certain fish under kapu during breeding seasons. They built a complicated system of fishponds to ensure a steady food supply for times when the gods were not with them. Fishermen today still leave offerings to the fish gods before casting their nets and lines or launching their boats. Ancient fishing shrines still dot Maui's coastline, surviving as sentinels that watch the sleek new charter fishing boats, armed with the latest nautical technology, head out to sea.

The ocean was also the playground of the ancients. Surfing began with the Hawaiians, who fashioned sleek boards from koa and wiliwili trees and rode the surf naked, in joy and exhilaration.

In varying degrees, the ocean still plays these roles. It washes up on sandy shorelines in explosions of foam or in gentle eddies. The oldest islands have the largest beaches. Maui's sands ring the island in a sparkling lei. Some beaches are completely isolated. Others are the jewels of glittering resorts, dotted with catamarans, windsurfers, Hobie cats, and floats.

The most popular beaches with local people are H.A. Baldwin Park with its famous bodysurfing shorebreak; Hookipa, where wind surfing was born on Maui, and both summer and winter swells roll in; and the three Kamaole parks at Kihei.

Long-time Island residents recognize the names Oneloa Beach and Puu Olai Beach. When Mainland hippies set up their tent cities at Makena in 1968, they called these neighboring sands Big Beach and Little Beach. Everyone else took to calling them, collectively, Hippie Beach. By 1972, the squatter population and the resultant problems necessitated eviction. The beaches, however, are still called Big and Little, and remain among the many undeveloped, wild and beautiful beaches of Maui.

Beyond the shoreline, the ocean is populated by a colorful collection of reef fish in iridescent garb of cerise, chartreuse, amber, turquoise, black, gold, and shades that have no name because linguists apparently are not divers, and the colors fade in seconds when the fish are lifted from the arms of the ocean. The sea's sequined residents are profusely on view to snorkelers at Kaanapali, Kapalua, and the point between Big and Little beaches. Offshore from Kihei is tiny Molokini island, a sliver of land like a quarter moon dropped into the ocean. Once an active volcano, it is now a broken bowl with one side missing. The ocean has entered the crater bringing along such a collection of reef fish that a snorkeler might feel as though he is swimming in a giant fish bowl.

Glass-bottom boats leave Lahaina harbor every day of the week for various coral beds and fish haunts. More ambitious explorers don scuba gear to discover some of the most spectacular marine scenery in the world. The Hawaiian Deep, a moat formed by the collapse of parts of the ocean floor surrounding the Hawaiian Islands, harbors creatures once thought to be legend, fish that resemble plants, and plants that look like visions of Martians.

Because much of Maui lies lower in the sea than at earlier times, magnificent sunken mountains and canyons, formed by volcanic action and later wind erosion, now are festooned in forests of coral.

Coral became an industry of note on the island in 1958, when the first beds of black coral were discovered. The black, the pink angel coral, and the very rare gold coral are fashioned with gold and other gems into jewelry treasured for its beauty and mystique.

Creatures great and small, named and unnamed, inhabit the reefs, the ranges, and the vast deep of Maui waters. Man enters Ka Moana, the ocean kingdom, only as a guest, but somehow, in a strange familial way, the sea becomes home. ■

Opposite: A surfer rides the "tube." —Erik Aeder. Previous page: Maui, with its steady tradewinds is a mecca for windsurfers from around the world. Once virtually unknown, Hookipa Beach became internationally famous for its combination of steady winds and good waves for jumping. —John Severson.

Above left: Daring windsurfer, Mike Eskimo, is caught in a graceful leap over the waves. —Sylvain Cazenave. Above right: Exhibiting championship form, Mitch Thorsen rides down the face of another Maui wave. —Sylvain Cazenave. Top: Windsurfers line up at Wailea for the start of the Maui to Molokini Island race. —Erik Aeder. Right: A young surfer paddles out over the reefs for his day's adventure. —Erik Aeder.

Left: Eagle rays swim in formation through the sunlit waters. —Ed Robinson.
Above: Ablaze in fiery pink and orange, this creature brightens the Maui depths. —Ed Robinson.
Top: Many varieties of coral populate the offshore reefs. —Ed Robinson. Previous
page: The beauty of Makena's "little beach" and "big beach" show that Maui
still has miles of deserted idyllic beaches. —Ray Mains.

213

Above: Crabbing is a great Maui pastime. —Carol Clarke. Top: The lion fish is one of the many curious finned creatures encountered on a Maui dive. —Ed Robinson. Right: The small island of Molokini, lying about three miles off the coast at Makena, offers excellent snorkeling and diving reefs. —Ray Mains. Previous page: A snorkeler, swimming in the shallow reefs of Molokini island enjoys a school of fish. —Ed Robinson.

*Left: A gentle giant, the whale shark, swims with a school of humans. —
Ed Robinson. Above: A diver appears to think twice before entering a dark sea cave. —David
Cornwell. Top: A striped Moorish idol leads the parade of jewel-toned fish. —Ed Robinson. Previous page:
A giant manta ray glides gracefully in the sea currents. —Pacific Whale Foundation.*

Maui's Special Visitors

*Leaping out of the water, a humpback
whale breaches off of the Maui coastline.-Left — Greg Kaufman. / Photographed from
underwater, whales are an awesome sight.-Below — Pacific Whale Foundation.*

"And God created great whales . . ."
— Genesis

There they are, mentioned by name in the Bible, along with Adam and Eve — top billing considering man's best friend and even the king of the beasts went unnoticed in the grand roll call of creation.

Of course, it would be difficult to ignore a whale. The blue whale is the largest animal that ever lived, six times as big as brontosaurus and weighing more than thirty elephants lashed together. The brain of the sperm whale weighs twenty pounds, four times more than a man's, and the frontal thinking part of the brain is extremely large although the purpose of this enormous cerebral mass is unknown.

The whale has social instincts and caring feelings similar to man's. They swim in herds or pods with mothers and children safely in the center. They have been observed to hold a wounded companion or calf afloat for days, even at peril of their own lives. Sperm whales have even been known to turn on their tormentors, ramming and sinking whaling boats.

Humpbacks, the type commonly seen off Maui from December until March, form fishing teams. Two will swim in a circle around a school of fish, blowing bubbles. When the fish become frightened and swim to the center of the bubble circle, the whales simply swim from underneath into the center of the bubble trap and swallow their dinner. Whales assist one another during childbirth: a "midwife" nudges the newborn infant to the surface for its first breath of air and then encourages it to nurse from its mother.

Whales are true warm-blooded mammals with lungs that breathe air, and with skin rather than gills. Their young are born live. The whale's "blowhole" is its nose, and the bones of a whale's flippers are much like a human hand. Approximately one hundred million years ago, whales lived on land. They are probably descendants of an early group of terrestrial mammals called creodonts, who were also the ancestors of dogs, cats, and seals.

There are two types of whales: the Odontoceti or toothed whales and the

223

Mysteceti or baleen whales. The sperm whale is the largest toothed whale, and its giant dental complex was prized by scrimshanders. Lahaina has become the center for this true American art form, dealing in both rare antique pieces and finely crafted new scrimshaw.

The largest of the baleen whales, which are mainly plankton eaters, is the one-hundred-foot blue. Humpbacks fall into the baleen category.

Man's relationship with this largest neighbor on the planet has been, at best, ambiguous. In ancient Greece, it was a serious crime to harm a dolphin. The Vietnamese regarded whales as guardian spirits, and a dead whale was accorded a burial fit for a king. The Hawaiians considered the whale to be the property of the king and was not to be touched by anyone else. The Phoenicians, on the other hand, launched the first whaling expeditions. Eskimo whaling villages go back to the time of Christ, and the Japanese have hunted whales for more than a thousand years. The Basques were the first to whale on a grand scale, organizing their hunting fleet as early as the twelfth century. By the early sixteenth century, whales had all but disappeared from European waters. There is speculation that Basque whalers were roaming as far as Newfoundland by the early sixteenth century.

The whale's real death knell was sounded, however, in 1868 when a Norwegian, Svend Foyn, invented the explosive harpoon gun which was mounted on steam-powered whaling boats. The Norwegians also developed the first factory ships, on board which whales could be fully processed while smaller satellite ships continued the hunt.

From 1825 to 1860, the height of the whaling era, there were fewer whales killed than from 1950 through 1955 when far fewer but technologically superior boats were involved.

The whale has been driven to the brink of extinction. As late as 1975, nobody even had a photograph of a whale. Forty thousand whales were killed that year.

Several organizations, including Greenpeace, the World Wildlife Fund, and the Pacific Whale Foundation, have been formed to save the whale and have succeeded in pressuring nations into signing treaties protecting the creatures. Some species are making a comeback. Some are not. Sadly the humpback, the joyous sixty-foot giant that frolics in the waters of Maui, is one whose numbers are not increasing.

The humpback is monogamous in its mating practices, and the female bears a calf once every two years. The young are born in Hawaiian waters where the whales come during the winter months, as the blubberless babes would freeze in their Arctic homes. The calves gain one hundred pounds a month, and at maturity may tip the scales at over one hundred thousand pounds.

The humpbacks communicate with one another through a complex chorus of song. The hauntingly beautiful melody seems to change every season, and the new composition is universally known among the whole tribe of whales. There is speculation that the sounds of boat engines interfere with the song transmission, and therefore with the intricate courting rituals of the humpback.

The song of the humpback has been recorded and may be heard aboard the brig *Carthaginian* moored in Lahaina harbor. This museum ship has been outfitted as a Yankee whaler. There is also a small whaling museum on Front Street in Lahaina, and an outdoor exhibit at Kaanapali Beach Resort. During the annual Marine Art Exhibit at Wailea in January and February, Maui's peak whale-watching season, the country's top marine artists donate part of the proceeds of their art sales to the Pacific Whale Foundation.

The whales themselves may be seen leaping clear out of the water in fantastic gymnastics all along the shoreline of Maui. It is an exhilarating spectacle. Hopefully, these gentle giants will survive to delight future generations. ■

Playground Mani

CHAPTER THIRTEEN

Maui is a natural playground. Its resorts resemble jewels, set with an artist's care in the green landscape beside the miles of glistening beaches.

The numerous golf courses are among the world's best and the playing is superb, despite the distractions of the surrounding scenery. Keeping an eye on the ball requires immense concentration when whales are cavorting in the offshore waves and rainbows crown the mountains in dazzling halos. The tennis courts, many lighted for night play, appear on equally glorious stages.

The island seriously entered the jet age of tourism in 1958, when Amfac, the century-old Hawaiian corporation, unveiled its Kaanapali Beach Resort, which has since become a model for resorts around the world.

Kaanapali is a three-mile scimitar of sand that had once been the playground of Hawaiian nobility. The kings and queens, who held court at Lahaina, would travel with enormous retinues to Kaanapali for royal luaus that would last for weeks. They would ride the long rollers on their huge eighteen-foot wooden surfboards, race their outrigger canoes, and fish in the bounteous waters. Royal children would play in the shallows while their attendants beat the bark of the mamake tree into fine tapa fabric for clothing and bedding. Where the Royal Kaanapali Golf Courses now carpet the low rounded hills, the ancient Hawaiians would compete in games of ulu maika, a form of lawn bowling; ku-po-lolu, or pole vaulting; swimming; and wrestling. In the evening, the awa, brewed from the root of the ti plant, would be poured and the beat of the ipu drums would reverberate in the gentle breezes, calling forth the dancers. In their chants, in the movements of their hands and their steps, in subtle nuances of gesture and glance, the dancers told their stories in magnificent hulas that celebrated heroic deeds, great voyages, and the genealogy of the kings, or they would slyly allude to known but unmentioned royal romances.

The gardens of the kings bloomed where the Royal Lahaina Hotel now stands. Former taro patches have become Acapulco-style swimming pools.

The goddess of fire, Pele, is said to have departed from Maui to dwell in Kilauea on Hawaii, from the site of the Sheraton Maui, at Puu Kekaa, now called Black Rock. Each evening at sunset, a young man reenacts the dramatic leaps of the warriors of old, particularly Kahekili. This king of Maui would mount Black Rock, face the dying sun, and leap into the sea, narrowly avoiding the jagged rocks, to emerge victorious over death, since Black Rock was considered to be the jumping off place of the spirit into the world beyond life.

Past Kaanapali, Kapalua sits on the fringes of the pineapple fields. Pioneered by Maui Land and Pineapple Company, the resort encompasses two golf courses, a tennis complex, a deluxe hotel, and residential and resort condominiums. An annual music festival in July draws musicians of international reputation and brings classical concerts to a place that mostly witnesses the hula.

At the other end of Maui, Alexander and Baldwin, another "Big Five" corporation, has developed the Wailea Beach Resort. Its imposing roster of resources includes five beaches, two major resort hotels, two golf courses, fourteen tennis courts, and two award-winning restaurants. Right next door at Makena, another jewel is being added to the lei of luxurious resorts strung on Maui's more than one hundred miles of magnificent coastline.

On the way to Wailea, the condominiums rising beside the sands of the Kihei beaches are a happy hodgepodge of sun, fun, and palm trees. They offer a seasonal chance at tropical living to those chained to less hospitable climates.

Whether the ingredients of an ideal vacation are the homey comforts of condo living, marble-halled hotels with waterfalls and parrots in the lobbies, a bungalow by the beach, or simply a pleasant room done up in wicker with a view and a refrigerator for the chablis, the dream becomes reality on Maui.

The dining choices are as wide as the blue Maui sky. Dinner may happen amid linen nappery, silver, and crystal, or with monkeypod bowls or paper plates. The occasion may call for forks, fingers, or chopsticks. Little French bistros dot the road, the elegant dining rooms of the resort hotels serve continental cuisine, and Maui's ethnic foods can be found everywhere. The luaus are as festive as in the days of kings, and feature, in addition to the pig and poi, an array of both the exotic and familiar.

Maui is fun country, whether by sunlight or moonlight and starlight. Sun-kissed, breeze-swept days invite the pursuit of pleasures that range from charterboat fishing, surfing, windsurfing, swimming, hiking, exploring, bicycle riding, horseback riding, and touring to just plain, no-apologies loafing. When the sun sets, maybe in a burst of emerald light called the Green Flash, Maui's flower-scented night opens its treasure-laden arms bearing moonstruck beaches for barefoot strolling, pulsating discos, lounges with romantic Hawaiian guitars, or a stage vibrating with the drums of Polynesia as hula dancers again captivate spellbound audiences and dramatic fire dancers leap through their smoky paces.

In such moments, the edges of time are sometimes blurred, and Maui the trickster, the wonder-worker, reigns again, lifting, rearranging, and disappearing, leaving in his wake the magic that only Maui can bestow on life. ∎

Opposite: A beach boy waiting to sign up fun seekers. A wide range of water activities and other sporting events are available at Maui's resorts. —Linny Morris. Previous page: Maui's crystal clear waters average 70° Farenheit and lure swimmers all year round. —Erik Aeder.

Left: Snorkelers explore the reef at Kaanapali. —Cliff Norager.
Above: Maui's sandy beaches are sunny all year long. —Linny Morris. Top:
Divers get ready for the deep. —David Davis.

231

Above left: Outrigger canoe paddling is a favorite water sport among local Maui residents and visitors. —Paul Chesley. Above right: Sailing excursion boats take to the sea daily. —Erik Aeder. Top: Tourists escape from colder weather, happy just for sunshine. —Erik Aeder.

Above: Bikini beauties have been judged and these are the winners.
—David Davis. Top left: the smile of a sun-bronzed girl is as warm as the Maui sunshine. —Erik Aeder.
Top right: Number twenty-four waits for the word. —David Davis.

Above: The Makena Surf is one of the last beachfront luxury condominiums in the Wailea area. Situated on the lower slopes of Haleakala crater in year round sunshine, the complex shares in the spectacular beaches and beautiful golf courses of the Wailea area. —Ray Mains.

Above: Pleasure boats bob at anchor. —Cliff Norager. Top: "Taking rays" is part of the Maui ritual. —David Davis. Previous pages: Seemingly sitting in a sea of lava, surfers shimmer in the last light of afternoon. —John Severson.

Kaanapali Beach Resort-Amfac's resort destination. The majestic West Maui Mountains are in the background fronted by sugar cane fields. Miles of sandy beach and clear calm water are the playground of over a million visitors a year.—Douglas Peebles

Above: Hula dancers silhouetted in the evening. —Gary Sohler.
Top: Evening comes gently to canoe paddlers and an oceangoing yacht anchored off Kaanapali. —Keith Collie. Right: A diver leaps from Black Rock, Kaanapali, every evening at sunset. —Cliff Hollenbeck.

*Above: The gallery watches at the Kapalua International Golf Tournament held annually
at the scenic Kapalua Golf Club. —John Severson.
Top: Resort sands are the perfect place for day dreams. —Linny Morris.
Left: A surfer heads home with the last light of day. —Randy Hufford.*

243

Above: The newly-opened Westin Maui, the resort of enchantment and unequaled beauty lies nestled upon Kaanapali Beach.   —David Zanzinger

*Above: Some of the regulars get in a game of serious beach volleyball.
—David Davis. Top: Maui tee-shirt philosophy has a certain wisdom. —Rita Ariyoshi. Right: Bathers
lounge in the offshore waters. —Cliff Norager.*

*Above: The elegant Hyatt Regency Maui
located on Kaanapali Beach.   —Hyatt Regency*

The grass tennis courts at Wailea, a resort area developed by Alexander and Baldwin, are among the most beautiful in the world. Wailea is located on the lower slopes of Haleakala, and sits on the white sandy beaches of Makena. —Alexander and Baldwin, Inc.

Above: The 18th hole at the Wailea Golf Course. —Ray Mains.
Top: The Stouffer Wailea Beach Resort. —Ray Mains. Right: The Maui Intercontinental
Wailea lies adjacent to beautiful Wailea Beach. —Ray Mains.

The beautiful Maui Marriott Resort, located on Kaanapali Beach, makes staying on Maui more than a vacation. The full range of amenities it offers to visitors makes it one of Maui's premier resorts. —Carl Shaneff